# 101 WAYS TO DEVELOP STU...

LB1065 .C27 1993

## DATE DUE

| | | |
|---|---|---|
| NO 18 '94 | | |
| MR 3 '95 | | |
| NO 3 '95 | | |
| MY 30 '96 | | |
| JY 18 '96 | | |
| DE 20 '96 | | |
| DE 19 97 | | |
| OC 16 '98 | | |
| DE 3 '98 | | |
| MY 27 '99 | | |
| NO 4 '99 | | |
| NO 23 01 | | |
| OC 20 05 | | |
| JE 8 05 | | |
| OC 19 08 | | |
| JE 23 08 | | |
| | | |
| | | |

DEMCO 38-296

# 101 Ways

## *to Develop Student Self-Esteem and Responsibility*

### Volume II

# 101 Ways

## to Develop
## Student Self-Esteem
## and Responsibility

### Volume II

*The Power to Succeed in School and Beyond*

**Frank Siccone**

Siccone Institute

**Jack Canfield**

Self-Esteem Seminars

**Allyn and Bacon**

*Boston   London   Toronto   Sydney   Tokyo   Singapore*

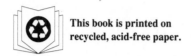

This book is printed on
recycled, acid-free paper.

**Library of Congress Cataloging-in-Publication Data**

Canfield, Jack, 1944–
    101 ways to develop student self-esteem and responsibility.
        p.      cm.
      v. 1. The teacher as coach / Jack Canfield and Frank Siccone — v.
    2. The power to succeed in school and beyond / Frank Siccone and
Jack Canfield.
      ISBN 0-205-14068-8 (pb)
      ISBN 0-205-14067-X (cb)
      1. Motivation in education.   2. Self-actualization (Psychology)
    3. Self-respect.  I. Siccone, Frank, 1948–  .  II. Title.
    III. Title: One hundred one ways to develop student self-esteem and responsibility.
    IV. Title: One hundred and one ways to develop
student self-esteem and responsibility.
    LB1065.C27   1993
    370.15'4—dc20                                  91-22997
                                                      CIP

Printed in the United States of America

10 9 8 7 6 5 4 3 2 1     96 95 94 93 92

# CONTENTS

──────────────── **Volume II** ────────────────

## Chapter Seven
## Social Responsibility: Classroom as Community   131

## Chapter Eight
## Community as Classroom   199

# PREFACE

*What we have found is that we're not preparing our children for the world of work.*

—William Brock
Chairperson, Commission on
Achieving Necessary Skills
U.S. Department of Labor

In its report, this special commission identified a foundation of skills and qualities designed to support workplace competencies. Among the skills listed were self-esteem, integrity, responsibility, self-management, communication and listening skills, decision making, and problem solving.

While some people may argue that schools have a broader purpose than just preparing students for future jobs, few could question the value of the above-mentioned skills for success in all aspects of life. So, whether we are talking about one's worklife or life's work, self-esteem and responsibility are essential components of happiness and success.

In creating this book we have sought to provide a sequence of activities that will help students discover that they have the power and skills necessary to achieve whatever they desire. Together with its companion volume, *The Teacher as Coach*, it is meant to be an extensive curriculum of 101 ways to develop student self-esteem and responsibility. *The Power to Succeed in School and Beyond* first takes students through a step-by-step process of uncovering the secrets of happiness and success. The principles taught through these lessons can be applied to their school studies, to their relationships with family and friends, to any area of their life where they want to be more effective.

The later sections of this volume explore the classroom as community and community as classroom. Students learn how to support one another in achieving goals and following through on commitments. They also practice ways of solving problems and managing conflict through communication and collaboration.

Through home, schoolwide and community-based projects students have opportunities to exercise their responsibility, develop their leadership skills, and expand their capacity to contribute to the world.

For us, every classroom represents the possibility of our working together with students—who are in fact the next generation of world citizens—to discover how to create a society in which everyone is esteemed, everyone accepts responsibility for themselves and each other, and everyone experiences success and happiness.

> *The purpose of education is to replace an empty mind with an open one.*
>
> —Malcolm Forbes

# Acknowledgments

## From Frank Siccone

This book represents for me a culmination of over fifteen years of articulating a practical philosophy of education for empowerment. I am grateful to Jack for his partnership in bringing this material to life in book form. His contributions were many; perhaps most impressive was his ability to translate abstract ideas into operational procedures.

Over the years, many people have made a difference to me and my work in innumerable ways. My earliest associates—from whom virtually all subsequent opportunities can be traced—are all acknowledged for their trust and extraordinary support of my vision: Thank you Jo Ann Bailey, Ricky Capsuto, Dorsey Davy, Michael Shipzner, Geneva Westendorf, Judy Wilkinson, and Esther Wright.

Special thanks to Joyce and Leon Spreyer, both for their extensive work on an earlier version of much of the material in this book, as well as for their many years of dedicated service. Others who helped with this book at its beginning stages are Chris Ducsai, Kris Krause, Linda Pearson, and Dean Muller.

Thanks, also, to Joe Fimiani and the special education administrators in Santa Clara County, Diane Stadler and the students at Vacaville High School, Robert Creer and the Richmond Unified School District students, John Tweten at San Jose Unified School District, Linda Kott and June Thompson from the California Association of Student Councils, and Hanoch McCarty and the National Council for Self-Esteem: all of whom made a direct contribution to this volume—either in the writing or field-testing of the activities.

Warmest appreciation to Dorothy J. Divack for her constant friendship, her quiet strength, her elegance and integrity, and for all the work she and her staff at the Center of Excellence did on preparing this manuscript. Acknowledgment is also due to Leslie Divack, Gayla Slikas, Faye Karnavy, and Gari Kloss for their help.

On a personal note, I want to express gratitude to my family for their love and encouragement, and to Chris Jehle for being such a wonderful person with whom to share my happiness and success.

## From Jack Canfield

Dr. Georgia Noble, my wife, for being responsible for our son Christopher while I worked long hours on this book.

Dr. John Enright, for modeling the context of responsibility so extraordinarily well.

Russell Bishop, for teaching me about being more accountable in many areas of my life.

Dr. Robert Resnick, who has been my therapist and my trainer, for introducing me to the basic ideas of $E + R = O$, and for modeling how to help people take more responsibility for their lives.

Dr. Jack Gibb, for teaching me to be responsible to my true self.

Martin Rutte, for teaching me how to confront irresponsibility in a compassionate way.

Larry Price and Kate Driesen, for being two of the most responsible people I know and for helping me develop some of these ideas as we cocreated the STAR (Success Through Action and Responsibility) Program for leaders in business and education.

Tim Piering, for being a teacher of personal power in my life and a constant pioneer in the technology of personal empowerment.

Bob Harris and Tere Baker Harris, for continually testing out my ideas and activities in their classrooms and seminars.

Martha Crampton, Phil Laut, Leonard Orr, and Sandra Ray, for what they have taught me about the use of affirmations and visualization.

John Vasconcellos, California State Assemblyman, for creating the California Task Force to Promote Self-Esteem and Personal and Social Responsibility. The existence of this task force and its excellent final report has made it much easier to promote our principles in schools all across the nation.

Patti Mitchell, for typing and retyping much of this manuscript.

These days it seems books are no longer simply written: they are produced by a great number of people. We especially want to thank the staff at Allyn and Bacon and BMR, who helped us mold our work into its final form.

Finally we want to thank all those teachers who have participated in our workshops and seminars, and who have used these activities in their classrooms and reported their experiences to us. Their feedback has been invaluable.

We have attempted to acknowledge throughout the text any individuals or organizations who have contributed an idea or an exercise to the curriculum. We also welcome your ideas and exercises so that we may expand and improve future editions. Please send your comments or questions to either of us:

Frank Siccone
Siccone Institute
2151 Union Street
San Francisco, CA 94123

Jack Canfield
Self-Esteem Seminars
6035 Bristol Parkway, Suite G
Culver City, CA 90230

# 101 Ways

## to Develop
## Student Self-Esteem
## and Responsibility

### Volume II

## PART III

# The True Purpose of Education

You can not teach a man anything. You can only help him discover it within himself.

—Galileo

# CHAPTER SIX

# Secrets of Happiness
# and Success

*He* *has achieved success who has lived well, laughed often,*
*and loved much; who has enjoyed the trust of pure women,*
*the respect of intelligent men and the love of little children;*
*who has filled his niche and accomplished his task; who has*
*left the world better than he found it, whether an improved*
*poppy, a perfect poem or a rescued soul; who has always*
*looked for the best in others, given them the best he had;*
*whose life was an inspiration; whose memory a benediction.*

—Bessie Anderson Stanley

# INTRODUCTION

*Success is getting what you want. Happiness is wanting what you get.*

—Anonymous

IN THIS CHAPTER, students get a chance to create a vision of what happiness and success mean to them, and learn some valuable tools for making their dreams come true.

The secrets of success and happiness that students will discover in this section include the following:

- the idea of working for what they want, rather than waiting for it to come along
- the power of knowing their purpose
- the steps of goal setting
- being responsible for discovering how things work so that they can get things to work for them
- the magic of making a commitment.

Each of these steps can be used any time students want to be successful. What the steps have in common is a focus on the student being in the driver's seat, being able to direct their own lives and being responsible for the results they produce.

As students increase the number of times they are successful, their self-esteem will also increase. They will appreciate themselves more as they watch themselves do what they say they are going to do, and realize the powerful effect they can have on their lives.

Students will even learn the secret of how never to "fail" at anything again.

## 54

# *Highlights of My Life*

## Purpose

This section of activities starts with an exercise that asks students to identify past experiences when they felt happy and successful. These then serve as the foundation for building future successes.

You may use this activity as a warm-up exercise, to energize students and promote interaction with their classmates.

## Procedure

1.  Hand out copies of the Highlights of My Life Worksheet.

2.  Ask students to divide their lives into thirds. For a 15-year-old, for example, the first third is from birth to age 5, the second third is from age 6 to 10, and the third is from age 11 to the present.

3.  Have students draw a picture in each frame representing a highlight event in their lives. Moments when they felt special or especially happy or successful are obvious choices.

4.  An alternative is for students to interview each other to fill in the highlights. In pairs, one student reports his or her highlights to a partner who records these moments on the first student's worksheet. Then they switch. Taking their worksheets with them, they get another partner for the second set of picture frames and repeat the process. A different partner is used for the third round.

5.  Students can then get into groups of six or eight to share their highlights one at a time.

# HIGHLIGHTS OF MY LIFE WORKSHEET

1st Third                                    As Recorded by: _____

2nd Third                                    As Recorded by: _____

3rd Third                                    As Recorded by: _____

# 55

# Highlights of My Life II

## Purpose

The purpose of this activity is for students to create a vision of what they would like to accomplish in the future.

## Procedure

1. You could do this activity solely as a worksheet exercise, using the same process as the previous activity, only this time asking the students to project 15 years into the future.

2. It could be done first as a guided visualization.

3. Introduce the activity by explaining what students will be doing:

   This activity is an eyes-closed, guided visualization. You will be in your favorite room watching a video of your life as it might be in the future. It is an opportunity for you to begin creating a successful future for yourself.

4. Ask students to close their eyes, relax, and take a few deep breaths.

5. Continue with the following instructions:

   You find yourself walking down a hallway that feels like home.

   At the end of the hallway, you discover a room just like the one you've always wanted.

   As you enter the room, you notice the colors in the room—the walls, the floor, and the furniture. You also notice that all your favorite things are in this room, and you realize this is really a perfect place to be.

   And now you decide to find a place where you can relax for a few

7

minutes—maybe a comfortable chair or sofa, or perhaps a bed or a stack of pillows on the floor.

As you get really comfortable, you decide to watch TV for awhile, and as you do, you notice a television set and you see that you have a good view of it from where you are sitting. . . . Very good!

As the television comes on, you see the title of a movie, Coming Attractions.

Your future is divided into three parts:

- the next five years,
- the five years after that, and
- the five years after that.

So you are reviewing the next 15 years of your life. You'll be seeing the highlights of your life—the major events or accomplishments that will occur during this time. Some events you may experience are:

- getting your driver's license, or your first car, or a new car
- graduating from high school, entering college, or getting a new job.

And now, as you continue to look and listen, notice what events unfold in your life.

If the screen goes blank or isn't clear, that's okay. Just ask yourself, 'What will I accomplish in my life during the next five years?' and see what comes up. Or ask yourself, 'What are some major events that are likely to happen over the next five years?' and listen to the answers. Just let it all flow easily. And as you do, you notice that you can see and hear many events you would like to have occur in the next five years.

*(Pause for two to four minutes.)*

And now you find yourself drifting even further into the future. You are beginning to move on to the next five years—6 to 10 years from now. Excellent! Very good!

By now you have probably graduated and been out of school or in college for awhile." *(Teacher: Use age-appropriate information here.)*

And, as you take your next breath, you begin to notice what high points might occur during this period of your life:

- maybe you'll be married or be in a significant relationship
- maybe you'll do some traveling to new places or move to another state
- maybe you'll get a new, more challenging job.

And, as I stop talking, you begin to see and hear what shows up on your screen.

*(Pause for two to four minutes.)*

Very good. . . . As you let go of these images, you begin to find yourself moving on to the 10- to 15-year range, so you might notice in the mirror how you've gotten a little older. You may be surprised at how much older and more mature you look!

During this time frame, you will be approaching and maybe passing 30 years of age. What will you have accomplished by now?

- a family of your own, perhaps
- owning your own home
- owning your own business
- maybe you've become famous for something.

Just let yourself continue to watch the screen and notice what you see ahead.

*(Pause for two to four minutes.)*

Very good. Now, as you begin to let go of these sounds and images, you find your awareness leaving the television set and coming back to the room. You realize that for now the movie is over. There'll be more to see later in the future, but it is time to leave now. So you get up and turn off the TV.

As you get ready to leave the room, you realize that you can always return here to go back to your future any time you want, simply by closing your eyes and walking down the hall, but for now it is time to leave.

As you leave and walk back down the hall, you realize what a gift it is to be clear about some of your visions for the future.

After awhile, you find yourself walking down the hallway to this classroom. As you enter the room, you take your seat and begin to notice how it feels to sit in your chair. You can feel your back against the back of the chair and your feet on the floor. As you notice the rising and falling of your chest and stomach as you breathe in and out, you become aware of the sounds around you in the room. You start to think about what this room looks like. When you have a clear sense of it, you slowly open your eyes and return your attention to the room.

6. Hand out copies of the worksheet, Highlights of My Life II, and have the students write or draw in the filmstrip frames images of their future success that they experienced during the fantasy.

7. Have the students share with partners or in their support groups.

8. Bring the entire class together for final comments.

1st Third                    As Recorded by: _____

2nd Third                    As Recorded by: _____

3rd Third                    As Recorded by: _____

*The future belongs to those who believe in the beauty of their dreams.*

—Eleanor Roosevelt

# Life Assessment Worksheet

## Purpose

In this chapter you and your students will learn techniques for achieving your goals—both short-term objectives and lifetime ambitions. That may sound like a lot of material for one chapter, but it really isn't very hard. There is a five-step process you'll learn for achieving success in whatever you set out to do.

You may have heard the old Chinese proverb "The journey of a thousand miles begins with a single step." But before you take the first step on your journey to success, there is something you have to do first—discover where you are right now!

The purpose of this activity is for students to do an honest assessment of what's working and what's not working in their lives as a baseline for setting goals for their future.

## Procedure

1. Ask students to fill out the Life Assessment Worksheet for homework.

2. The following day, have them get into a group with four other people and take turns discussing their answers with the group. Give each student three to five minutes in which to share. (The amount of time should be based on the students' verbal ability. Use a stopwatch and tell students when to switch to the next person. This assures that everyone will get equal time.)

3. After everyone has discussed the answers to the questionnaire, have them take turns sharing their goals—the last question on page 18.

4. As they listen to the others explain their goals, they may ask each other questions that will help them become clearer on exactly what they want to accomplish and how this class will help them do so. (Allow about one to two minutes per student.)

5. Next, they are to identify the first step on the journey toward their goal and make agreements with their support groups to take this action during the next 24 hours. Monitor the time to assure that each group ends on time, and each student has a chance to share (about one to two minutes per student).

# LIFE ASSESSMENT WORKSHEET

On a scale of 1 to 10 (1 = low, 10 = high), how well is your life working? How satisfied are you with the way things are in your life right now? How do you feel about the following areas?

- yourself                                                    _____

- your relationships with your friends       _____

- your relationships at home                      _____

- your performance at school                    _____

- outside interests, talents, hobbies, sports   _____

- other areas of your life (please list)

_____          _____

_____          _____

_____          _____

In each of the following areas, write things that *are* going well:

How you feel about yourself _____

_____

_____

Your relationships with friends _____

_____

_____

Your relationships at home _____

_____

_____

Your performance at school _____

_____

_____

Outside interests, talents, hobbies, sports _____

_____

_____

Other areas of your life _____

_____

_____

In each of the following areas, write things that are *not* going so well:

How you feel about yourself _____

_____

_____

Your relationships with friends _____

_____

_____

Your relationships at home _____

_____

_____

Your performance at school _____

_____

_____

Outside interests, talents, hobbies, sports _____

_____

_____

Other areas of your life _____

_____

_____

Now, using the answers you gave to the preceding questions, identify the areas you would like to focus on in this class. They may be weak areas that need improvement as well as strong areas you want to make even stronger.

Areas of my life I want to work on in this class:

_____

_____

_____

_____

_____

_____

Select one area that is most important to you, and write a goal for yourself.

_____

_____

_____

_____

Identify the first step—one action you can take in the next 24 hours—toward achieving your goal.

_____

_____

_____

_____

**18**

*The* great end of life is not knowledge but action.

—Thomas Henry Huxley

You want to be <u>happy</u>? What kind of goal is that?!!

Courtesy of Gail Machlis

# Success and Happiness Collage

> $O$*ne can never consent to creep when one feels an impulse to soar.*
>
> —Helen Keller, *The Story of My Life*

## Purpose

When you dream of success, what do you see? Do you imagine yourself winning the lottery? Do you see yourself in a position of power and influence? Do you have a picture of your ideal home and family? Or do you dream of making an enduring mark in the world? Or being remembered for your contribution to humanity?

One secret to being successful is to have a clear picture of what success looks like for you. The next two activities are designed to have your students develop detailed pictures of what they want in the way of success and happiness.

## Materials Needed

- heavy drawing paper (12 × 18 inches)

21

- magazines
- scissors
- glue or paste

## Procedure

1. Distribute to students the drawing paper, magazines, scissors, and glue. They may work in groups to share some of the materials.

2. Tell students to look through the magazines and find pictures of things that suggest what they personally think of as success and happiness.

3. Have them cut out pictures and glue them on the paper in designs that represent their personal views of success and happiness.

4. Suggest that they include words or phrases that fit into their designs. If there are other images they want to include that they can't find in magazines, they are free to draw them.

5. When the students have completed their collages, have them get into groups of four (or their support groups) and take turns showing the others their collages and explaining how the designs illustrate their ideas of happiness and success. The other group members may ask questions if anything on a design seems unclear.

6. You may want to close the activity with a full class discussion along the following lines: "Look again at the collage you created. Of all the images you used in the design, which is most important to you? How does the image relate to the things you said you wanted to focus on in this class? See your answers to the 'Life Assessment Questionnaire.' How many of the pictures are the same as those you drew in the 'Highlights of Your Life' activity?"

7. You may want to invite your students to take their collages home, and find time to discuss them with one or both of their parents. The collage can be used as a starting point for them to let their parents know what their current life goals are.

8. You may also want to make the following suggestions: "Ask your parents to tell you what their goals were when they were your age. Then find out what they would like to see for your future. See if your goals and your parents' goals for you match."

9. Ask your students to bring the collages back to class so that they can be displayed on the bulletin board.

# Success and Happiness Visualization

## Purpose

This activity supports students' success by having them visualize achieving their goals.

## Procedure

1. Introduce the activity by saying:

   Today, you'll add some more detail to your picture of happiness and success. The collage you made during the previous activity included some of the symbols you identify with success and happiness. Today's eyes-closed visualization lets you 'put yourself in the picture' and feel what it's like to make your dreams come true.

2. Now read the following instructions for the eyes-closed visualization process:

   Please close your eyes, relax, and take a few deep breaths.

   Visualize walking down the hall to your favorite room, the room you created before with all your favorite things in it. . . .

   Return to the place where you can sit comfortably to watch TV . . . that chair, the sofa, bed, or pillows where you fully relax and just watch your television. . . .

   Once again, you'll be spending a few minutes watching some pictures on the TV screen, so make sure that you have a good view. . . .

With your remote control device, go ahead and turn on the TV and the VCR.

Today you are going to watch a video entitled *Lifestyles of the Successful and Happy*.

As the video begins, you first see the pictures that you cut out of the magazine when you did your success and happiness collage.

As you remember the images you found that represented being happy and successful, you now see these same images on the TV screen.

Now you begin to see yourself on the TV amid these images of happiness and success.

If your pictures were of objects, you see yourself holding the objects . . . and

If your pictures were of places, you see yourself in these places. . . .

And if your pictures were of people, you see yourself with these people. (*Pause*.)

Now, you notice that the remote control of the VCR has a special button (very advanced technology) a 3-D button that will change the picture from being two-dimensional on the TV screen to being three-dimensional, so that you can actually walk around the objects . . . and see them from all sides . . . and touch them. . . .

So, as you push the 3-D button, you experience yourself actually surrounded by your images of happiness and success. You can:

• put on the clothes you want
• drive that car
• live in your home
• walk along the beach at your vacation resort.

As you interact with each of these things and people, you experience the happiness that you have interacting with other people . . . with your friends . . . and with your family.

The longer you do this, the more alive and real these pictures become for you.

Notice how you can easily project those feelings of happiness and success now. . . .

Very good. And now bring into your experience the thoughts, emotions, and physical sensations that go along with being happy and successful, having achieved all your goals.

Okay, you'll have another minute now to just enjoy this experience before returning back here.

(*Wait one minute*.)

Okay, as you realize that this experience of happiness and success is available to you at any time simply by coming to your special room and watching this special 3-D video, you also realize that it is time to leave now, so you press the 3-D button on the remote control and switch back to sitting in the chair with the pictures on the TV. . . . Very good.

As you turn off the VCR and TV, you stand up and get ready to leave your favorite room for now. Remember, you can always return to this favorite room simply by closing your eyes. . . . But for now imagine coming back into the hallway, walking back into this room. Recall what this room looks like; where you are; who else is here. Bring yourself into this room totally. Let yourself feel good about being here. When you know you are back in this room totally and feel good about being here, please open your eyes.

3. After the visualization, have your students join their groups to share their experience. Suggest that they describe what they pictured about success and happiness during the eyes-closed process. Were there any surprises? What did it feel like to be that happy and successful? Give each student three to five minutes to share.

**PEANUTS**/Charles Schulz

# Secret Number 1: GROE
# Get Rid of Expectations

## Purpose

This activity is designed to help students gain the insight that their active involvement is crucial to their success. This activity is continued the next day in Activity 60, "Setup for Upset." Please read that activity *before* doing this one.

## Materials Needed

- butcher paper
- markers

## Procedure

1. Write on the chalkboard "Secret Number 1: GROE." Tell your students that they will figure out the secret by the end of tomorrow's activity.

2. Engage your students in the following discussion:

   Do you know the word *spectator*?

   A spectator is a person who watches other people perform, like a spectator sitting in the stands at a football game.

   How about the word *spectacles*?

A spectacle is something that you watch such as a football game and *spectacles* is another name for eyeglasses.

Both these words—*spectator* and *spectacles*—come from the same Latin root word as does *expectations,* and both are connected with its meaning.

*Expectation* means to sit back—like a spectator—and wait for someone else to make things happen. When you have an expectation about how something is going to turn out, you are looking at the event through your expectations, as though you were peering through a pair of glasses.

What happens when you expect something to happen and it doesn't turn out? Usually, you are disappointed. The reality doesn't match up with the idea in your head of how it ought to be. That's one of the problems with having expectations. When you approach situations with a lot of expectations, you're likely to have a lot of disappointments. (The word *disappointment* means that I make an 'appointment' in my mind that the future doesn't keep.)

Another problem with expectations is that you aren't in control. You're sort of sitting around waiting for something to happen or for someone to do something. Having expectations is an irresponsible way to live; you're looking outside of yourself for the source of the action instead of taking charge yourself.

3. Ask the students to get a piece of paper and a pencil.

4. Tell them to write down their expectations by completing each of the following sentence stubs:

   • "Relative to how I will do in this class, I expect . . ."
   • "Relative to how successful I will be in school, I expect . . ."
   • "Relative to what I will do after I graduate, I expect . . ."
   • "Relative to a job or career, I expect . . ."
   • "Relative to having a family, I expect . . ."
   • "Relative to having money and financial success, I expect . . ."
   • "Relative to living a fulfilled life, I expect . . ."

5. Tell them to write down their expectations in sentences, starting with the words "I expect . . ."

6. After they have finished their lists of expectations, have them form groups of five and go over each others' lists of expectations, noticing similarities and differences.

7. Next give each group a large piece of butcher paper, to write a group list of expectations. Group members are to include on their paper any expectations that appeared on more than one person's list, as well as any other expectations the group thought were important.

8. After students complete their group lists, hang them up on the wall.

9. Then say to your class, "Now for some fun! You've been working really hard in this class so far, and you deserve a break. Right? For being such a hard-working class, you can expect a party tomorrow as your reward."

10. "Get back into your groups and make a wish list of things you'd like to have at the party—what kind of food, what to drink, music, decorations, whatever you expect to find at a good party."

11. At the end of class, collect their wish lists.

**PEANUTS** /Charles Schulz

3-3   © 1988 United Feature Syndicate, Inc.

# 60

# Setup for Upset

## Purpose

This activity is designed to allow your students to experience the consequence of only having expectations and not acting to realize them.

## Procedure

1. Group the class into a circle.

2. Go around the circle and find out what is happening about having a party. Ask:

   - "How many people are expecting to have a party today?"
   - "How many people brought things for the party?"
   - "What did you bring? How much?"
   - "Is there enough of what you need to actually have a party?"

3. "If so, congratulations! You are such an enlightened group that you deserve a party. ENJOY!"

4. "If not, what happened?"

   - "Did having expectations get you what you wanted?"
   - "Why not?"
   - "If having expectations didn't get you a party, is it likely that having expectations will get you the other things you say you want in life?"
   - "Expectations can set you up for an upset if you think they're going

to happen but don't do anything about making them come true. (By the way, the same thing is true about hoping and wishing. They are just expectations with different names.)"

- "Expectations are irresponsible because when you expect something to happen you are looking outside yourself for the source of the action. Your role is that of a spectator, waiting to see if someone else is going to deliver."
- "A more responsible way to get what you want is to change your expectations into intentions. An intention is a specific plan of action that *you* put into motion."

5. Ask the students to get back into their groups. Start with the list of expectations they wrote, as groups, on the butcher paper. Knowing what they now know about expectations, have them rewrite each expectation into an intention. If they have no intention of doing anything about the expectation, cross it off the list. Chances are it won't happen.

6. Now have them go back to the list of expectations they each wrote personally during the previous session and cross off the unimportant expectations—the ones they don't feel like doing anything about. Then have them change the important expectations into intentions. To do this, they restate the expectation so that *they* are the person who acts to make it happen.

**Example of expectation:** "I expect to graduate."
**Translated into intention:** "I intend to earn the units required to graduate by studying and handing in all my assignments."

7. When they have finished translating their expectations into intentions, bring the whole class together.

8. Go around the class having each student share one expectation he or she had that has now been turned into an intention. Have them use the following structure, which you may want to write on the chalkboard: "My expectation was _____. My intention is _____."

9. Before they leave class today, let them decide as a group what they want to *do* about having a party. If they are willing to be responsible for making it happen, let them plan one that will work for you as well.

10. Tell them that Secret Number 1, GROE, means "Get Rid Of Expectations."

**W**ork out your own salvation. Do not depend on others.

—Buddha

# Calvin and Hobbes

by Bill Watterson

WATERSON 11·10 ©1989 Universal Press Syndicate

# 61

# Secret Number 2: $S = P \times C$
# Satisfaction = Purpose × Clarity

*This is the true joy in life: the being used for a purpose recognized by yourself as a mighty one. The being a force of nature instead of a feverish selfish little clot of ailments and grievances, complaining that the world will not devote itself to making you happy.*

*Life is no brief candle to me. It is a sort of splendid torch which I have a hold of for the moment . . . and I want to make it burn as brightly as possible before handing it on to future generations.*

—George Bernard Shaw

## Purpose

There is a familiar story about three bricklayers who were working on a job. A man passed by and asked the first one what he was doing. "Can't you see, you fool? I'm laying bricks!" was the reply.

The man approached the second worker and asked what he was doing. "Me?" said the bricklayer. "I'm building a wall."

Finally, the passer-by reached the third worker, who seemed to be doing work of a much higher quality than either of the others. "What are you doing?" asked the passerby.

"What I am doing," the man answered with a radiant smile on his face, "is creating a magnificent cathedral!"

The point of the story is that having a purpose—knowing what end point you have in mind—is what gives your work its meaning and value. The mightier the purpose, the greater the satisfaction.

Part of our responsibility as educators is to make learning relevant to students by helping them see their purpose for being in school. This is the purpose of this activity.


## Procedure

1. Write on the chalkboard "Secret Number 2: $S = P \times C$." Let the students know that they will discover what this means at the end of the activity.

2. Have students take out pencils and paper.

3. Ask them to write a one-sentence statement of the purpose of school, as they understand it. Suggest that they start their sentences, "The purpose of school is . . ."

4. After they have written their statements, instruct them each to find a partner.

5. After comparing statements with each other, partners are to select one of the statements or write a new statement that they both agree is the best way to describe the purpose of school.

6. When all have selected or created their statements, have all the pairs join up with other pairs to make foursomes.

7. Once again, they are to compare their two statements, and as a group, select one statement or write a new one that they all agree on.

8. Now, these four join up with another foursome to make a group of eight. Repeat the process.

9. Next, join them together to make a group of 16. Repeat the process.

10. Finally, come together as a whole class. Read the two statements the groups defined, and form a final statement on the purpose of school.

11. Have someone print the "purpose of school" statement on a piece of butcher paper or poster board.

12. Next, lead the class in a discussion as suggested here:

- "Think about your various classes, assignments, and activities."
- "Do all of them make sense in terms of the purpose of school as you have defined it?"
- "Are there any of your school activities that don't have meaning for you as they relate to this statement of purpose?"
- "Was there a time when these activities might have been more relevant?"
- "Are there any other things you think you ought to be doing at school that would be more in keeping with your purpose?"
- "What does all this mean to you personally, and how you can apply yourself to school?"

13. End the session with a discussion of Secret Number 2: $S = P \times C$, Satisfaction = Purpose × Clarity.

## DENNIS THE MENACE

"THE TROUBLE WITH LEARNING IS THAT IT'S ALWAYS ABOUT STUFF YOU DON'T KNOW."

# Life Purpose Fantasy

## Purpose

Just as activities need a purpose to give them meaning, so too people must have a purpose. Without purpose, life becomes pointless, repetitive, and dull.

But even though having a purpose is so important to people's happiness, surprisingly few people make the effort to consciously think through and formulate a statement of purpose for their lives. In this process your students will have a chance to do just that!

The Life Purpose Fantasy provides the answer to a central question when dealing with potential and inner validation. Before doing the visualization, conduct a discussion of what is meant by the term "life purpose." You may want to brainstorm what this concept means to your students. The usual pre-session comments are very career related and quite different from the post-session comments.

## Materials Needed

- drawing paper
- colored markers or crayons

## Procedure

1. To begin, ask the students to get into a comfortable position with their spines straight, either sitting up or lying down. Then ask them

to close their eyes and become relaxed, being aware of the rhythm of their inhalation and exhalation.

**2.** Begin the fantasy by saying:

We are about to review your life.

As you take your next breath you will begin to experience yourself going backward in time.

You begin by thinking about this day.

Go back to when you woke up this morning. . . .

And you think about what you have done all day . . . today?

Now, you look back at the past week . . . and then the past month . . . and now the past year. . . .

You just keep reviewing the significant events of this past year. . . .

What did you look like? . . .

Whom were you with? . . .

Where did you go? . . .

As you review these past events you are able to avoid judging or getting caught up with any particular event. . . .

You just allow your life to pass by as if you were watching a movie . . . Very good.

Now, you let yourself go back to your previous grade . . . and then . . .

To your elementary grades . . .

To the primary grades . . .

To the time you first entered school . . .

To being a young child . . .

A two-year old . . .

A baby . . .

To the time of your birth and the time you were in your mother's womb. . . .

And now go back to the time before your conception. . . .

You realize you are about to meet a special guide. . . .

As this guide appears and you look into his or her eyes, you feel your guide's unconditional love and strength and beauty. . . .

As you take in this experience you just let whatever happens happen. . . .

39

And now you realize it is time to communicate with your guide in whatever way feels right to you. . . .

And so you ask your guide, 'what is my life purpose?' . . .

As the guide begins to speak, you simply listen to your guide's response.

*(long pause . . .)*

And having heard these words, you now notice what you are experiencing.

And now the guide tells you that it is time to begin your journey back through time and space.

And so you say farewell to your guide, knowing you may visit your guide at any time.

And now you begin to make your journey back, bringing with you your awareness of your life purpose.

You find that it is easy to make your journey back through time, through your birth . . .

Back through your infancy . . .

And then your childhood . . .

And finally to the present moment in this room.

When you are ready, just take a few deep breaths and then open your eyes. Very good.

Please remain silent and simply draw and write about your experience.

We will share our journey after a few minutes.

3.  When they open their eyes, give them art paper and colored markers and have them write the message they received and draw the images they visualized.

4.  Move the class into small groups and ask each student to take turns describing his or her experience of the visualization while sharing the drawing with the group.

    The responses to this work have covered a wide range of expression. The drawings have contained many powerful and moving archetypal symbols such as light, rainbows, the sun, contact with another being, flowing robes, mountains, meadows, flowers, animals, and so on. The writing has been poetic, creative, beautifully simplistic, and yet full and rich, as in the following responses:

    • I felt like I was in a very special place. Everything was very clear. I could relate to my guide quite well. It was like being in heaven.

• When I met my guide and asked my question, he gave me a great big smile and held my hands. It was like he was saying, 'It's real neat. Try it. It's a great thing to be a person.' He gave me a sense of wanting to be, just by holding my hands. My guide seemed like a real nice person, the kind people would like to know. When we were holding hands I thought, 'Wow, I hope everyone's like this.' When I was leaving, I looked back. It seemed as though he was saying, 'It's okay. Go ahead,' just by looking at me. We met in a place full of nothingness.

# Life Purpose Fantasy II

## Purpose

You may use this visualization instead of, or in addition to, the previous activity.

## Procedure

1. Ask students to get into a comfortable position with their spines straight, either sitting up or lying down. Then ask them to close their eyes and become relaxed, being aware of their breathing. Ask them to take a few deep breaths.

2. Begin the fantasy using the following script:

   Imagine yourself walking down a road toward a beach.

   As you approach the beach area, you feel the sun on your face and your arms.

   You can notice the colors and hear the various sounds that are there.

   Can you hear the ocean as you get closer?

   As you step onto the sand, you may want to take your shoes off and feel the sand under your feet and between your toes.

   Does the sand feel warm or cool?

   As you look around, you find a place on the beach where you can sit down and be alone for awhile.

   Perhaps you pick a place near where the sand meets the ocean so that you can watch the waves come rolling in.

   As you watch the waves, you observe the ebb and flow of the tides—the ever constant movement of the water.

As you are sitting there on the beach, you notice a large seashell nearby—the kind that you can hold up to your ear and hear the sound of the ocean in.

Only this is a special seashell. It has a special message for you—a message related to your purpose in life.

As you pick up this shell and hold it to your ear and listen, you begin to hear something—a sound, a word, a phrase, a message that reveals something to you about your purpose in life—what your life is all about, the meaning of your existence, your reason for being on earth.

Listen . . .

And now you find yourself nodding your head, but only after you hear this special message and remember it . . . *(Long pause.)* . . . Very good!

And now as you put the shell down and relax, you begin to watch the waves again.

And, as you do, you notice that coming in on one of the waves there appears to be an old bottle.

Yes, you see that it is a bottle and it looks as if there is a piece of paper or something in it.

And as you continue to watch it, the bottle is washed up onto the shore by the waves.

As it rolls up near you, you reach down and pick it up.

As you hold the bottle in your hand, you can feel that it has been worn smooth by the years at sea.

As you look into the bottle, you can see that it contains a message—and the message is for you.

You realize that once again, it is related to your purpose in life—your special mission here on earth.

And so you go ahead and take the message out of the bottle and read it. Notice what it says and what it means to you. . . . *(Pause.)*

As you once again commit this message to memory, you put the bottle down and as you do you find your eye is attracted to a stick in the sand.

There seems to be something unusual about this stick, almost as if it were a magic stick.

As you pick up the stick, you notice that it wants to write something in the sand.

As you point the end of the stick, it is sort of moving on its own—writing some kind of message in the sand.

As you let the stick move freely, you see that it spells out another message for you about your purpose in life.

When the stick is finished, you stand back and read what the stick has written. . . . *(Pause.)*

And you realize that each message you have received has given you more and more clarity about your life purpose.

As you think more deeply about this message, you find a place where you can sit down and be comfortable again.

As you relax for a moment, you reflect on the three messages you have received so far and what they mean to you. . . . *(Long pause.)*

As you look up, you notice a very wise-looking person walking down the beach.

You have the feeling you know this person.

You recognize this person to be your special guide—someone who knows you and loves you very deeply.

As you invite this guide to sit down with you, you notice how safe and peaceful you feel in this person's presence.

Since this person is very wise and has been sent as your special guide, you have an opportunity to ask this person any questions that you have about your purpose in life and anything else you want to know.

So just go ahead and talk with your guide and listen carefully to the wisdom being shared with you at this time. . . . *(Long pause.)*

Very good. Your guide tells you that it is time to leave now, but that you can get in contact any time you want to simply by closing your eyes and coming to this beach.

Any time you feel the need for guidance, your guide will be there ready to help you.

So for now you say thank you and goodbye, and you get ready to leave the beach.

Moving slowly, you stand up, brush off the sand from your clothes and start walking to the school.

If you've taken your shoes off, you take a minute to put them back on now and then continue your walk to the school.

As you enter the school, you walk down the hall until you come to our classroom.

Visualize yourself walking back into this room. . . .

Remember what the room looks like. . . .

Remember where you are in the room and who else is here. . . .

Come back now into this room totally and allow yourself to feel good about being here.

When you know you are back here fully and feel good about being here, open your eyes.

3. Ask the students to draw and write about their experience for five minutes.

4. Ask them to get into their support groups and share the experience with their group. Give each student three to five minutes to share.

5. You may want to finish by sharing and taking questions with the whole class.

## 63

# *The Epitaph*

## Purpose

This activity reinforces the life purpose exercises and is designed to have students reflect on what is really important in life.

## Materials Needed

Art supplies such as art paper or cardboard, markers or materials for papier-mâché.

## Procedure

1. Introduce the activity by discussing what an epitaph is, as follows: "Have you ever gone to a cemetery and read the engravings on the tombstones? In olden days, people used to write sayings, called *epitaphs,* to be put on their tombstones as a way of summing up their lives. Some of these contained grim humor—a last dig at people they thought made their lives miserable. For example:

    *Here lies the body of Mary Ford,*
    *Whose soul, we trust, is with the Lord;*
    *But if for hell she's changed this life,*
    *'Tis better than being John Ford's wife.*

    "Other epitaphs expressed the personal style and beliefs of the departed. A well-known example is Benjamin Franklin's epitaph:

*The Body*
*of*
*Benjamin Franklin, Printer*
*(Like the cover of an old book,*
*Its contents torn out,*
*And stript of its lettering and gilding),*
*Lies food for worms.*
*Yet the work itself shall not be lost,*
*For it will (as he believed) appear once more,*
*In a new*
*And more beautiful edition,*
*Corrected and amended*
*by*
*The Author.*

"Although Ben Franklin is known for many accomplishments, he chose to describe himself as a printer. Notice how he compares himself to an old book, which will reappear in a new and improved edition, which The Author (meaning God) will correct.

"The value of writing an epitaph is that it makes you think of what's really important about your life that you want to leave behind for future generations."

2.  Have the students get a piece of paper.

3.  Ask them to answer this question as though they were at the last day of their lives, looking back on all they had done: "If there were one sentence that summarized the meaning of your life and the contribution you made to the world, what would that sentence say?"

4.  "Now, looking at the sentence you wrote, decide what you want to put into your epitaph. It may be written in the form of a poem, but it doesn't have to be. Your one sentence already may say exactly what you want engraved on your tombstone."

5.  After they have their epitaph, have them get into groups of five and take turns sharing their epitaphs. They are to explain what their epitaphs mean or represent, and as they listen to the epitaphs of other people they may ask questions and make suggestions that seem appropriate.

6.  Now have them get materials to make tombstones. This can be done

on cardboard, with papier-mâché, or simply drawn on art paper. They are to inscribe their epitaphs on the tombstones.

7. When they are finished, they are to bring their tombstones to the class circle to share with the class what they created, and explain the significance of their epitaphs.

8. Final discussion may include responses to these questions:

- "What is the connection between your epitaph and the purpose of your life that you identified in the visualization process?"
- "If you knew that for some reason your life were going to end in 24 hours, how would you spend this last day of your life?"
- "What would be the most important things for you to accomplish?"
- "What could you do to ensure that your life purpose and your epitaph were being fulfilled?"

**Note:** *It is a good idea for you also to participate in this activity and prepare your own epitaph as an example for the students.*

*Also, do not do this exercise if someone in class has recently had a relative or friend die. It could stir up unpleasant memories and unexpressed grief. Be sensitive to the possible morbid aspects of kids writing their own epitaphs. If teenagers with whom you are working are suicide prone, this would also be an unwise activity to use.*

## Make It Come True

*In 1957, a ten-year-old boy in California set a goal!!! At the time, Jim Brown was the greatest running back ever to play pro football, and this tall, skinny boy wanted his autograph. In order to accomplish his goal, the young boy had to overcome some obstacles.*

*He grew up in the ghetto; he never got enough to eat. Malnutrition took its toll, and a disease called rickets forced him to wear steel splints to support his skinny, bowed-out legs. He had no money to buy a ticket so he waited patiently near the locker room until the game ended and Jim Brown left the field. He politely asked Brown for his autograph. As Brown signed, the boy explained, "Mr. Brown, I have your picture on my wall. I know you hold all the records. You're my idol."*

*Brown smiled and began to leave, but the young boy wasn't finished. He proclaimed, "Mr. Brown, one day I'm going to break every record you hold!" Brown was impressed and asked, "What is your name, son?"*

*The boy replied, "Orenthal James. My friends call me O. J."*

*O. J. Simpson went on to break all but three of the rushing records held by Jim Brown before injuries shortened his football career. Goal setting is the strongest force for human motivation. Set a goal and make it come true.*

—Dan Clark

**64**

# Secret Number 3:
# WIN With INtention

> *S*uccess is not the result of spontaneous
> combustion. You must set yourself on fire.
>
> —Reggie Leach

## Purpose

The purpose of this activity is to empower students to be successful by
having them learn about the importance of setting goals.

## Procedure

1. Introduce the activity by leading the following discussion.
   "So far you have learned two important terms related to having
   success and happiness in your life.

   "The first term is EXPECTATIONS. As you may remember, expectations turned out to be an irresponsible and not very effective
   way of getting what you want. The important point about ex-

pectations is that we all have them. When you realize you are approaching a situation with expectations, translate them into intentions to take charge of creating the outcomes you want. Who remembers Secret Number 1? (GROE) How about Secret Number 2? ($S = P \times C$.)

"Your PURPOSE is an ongoing general statement that usually defines your direction for a lifetime or at least for a long period of time. Here is an example of a purpose statement:

'My purpose in life is to influence people to preserve the environment and save animal species from extinction.'

GOAL is another way of saying *intention*. It is a statement of a specific result you want to achieve. This is a goal statement:

'My goal is to major in environmental studies in college and later earn a doctoral degree, and get a job with the Wildlife Federation.'

"You're probably already familiar with the word *goals*. Where would soccer be without them? How would your favorite football team make touchdowns without a goal line? You need a goal line in order to know in which direction to run. But what about in your own life? Do you set goals for yourself? Do you know what to do to accomplish your goals? Here is an important secret about goals."

2. Write on the chalkboard "Secret Number 3: WIN." Tell them that if they don't know what this stands for, they will soon.

3. Have the class brainstorm a list of goals any of them have ever set for themselves and achieved. Have someone write the list on the board.

4. Once they have their brainstormed list, let them look it over and come up with a working definition of the word *goal*.

5. Now break them up into groups of five students each.

6. Have them take turns reviewing with their groups the goal they set for themselves in Activity 56 Worksheet, "Life Assessment." They are to let their groups know how well they each are doing in accomplishing their individual goals.

7. Bring them back together again as a total class and have them report on what each group discussed. In closing, you may want to make the following suggestions:

- "Congratulate yourself on your progress. If there are any areas in which you are not moving toward your goals, write down what is getting in the way and what you can do about it."

- "What can you do in the next 24 hours to move forward on one of your goals? Identify a specific action to take, set a time for achieving it, and decide exactly how you are going to proceed. Then, DO IT."

8.  Now refer back to "Secret Number 3." Tell them that WIN means "With INtention."

---

*I*'m not old enough to play baseball or football. I'm not eight, yet. My mom told me when you start baseball, you aren't going to be able to run that fast because you had an operation. I told mom I wouldn't need to run that fast. When I play baseball, I'll hit them out of the park. Then I'll be able to walk.

—Direct quote from a 7-year-old*

---

*Edward J. Mcgrath, Jr., *An Exceptional View of Life* (A Child: Point of View Publication. Distributed by the Easter Seal Society. Library of Congress #77-73684 1977).

*The* highest reward for a person's toil is not
what they get for it, but what they become by it.

—John Ruskin

**MISTER BOFFO** By Joe Martin

# 65

# Long Term, Short Term

## Purpose

The purpose of this activity is to help students translate their life purpose into long-term and short-term goals.

## Procedure

1. Have students get a pencil and distribute copies of the four-page Long Term, Short Term Worksheet.

2. Inform them that this activity will be timed, so they need to listen for the signal to start and stop.

3. Proceed with these instructions:

   - "When I give you the signal to begin, write down your lifetime goals. These are things you want to accomplish sometime during your life.
   - "They may be related to your job, career, or profession; to your family and friends; to money, lifestyle, and personal possessions; to important things you want to achieve; or to ways you want to enjoy yourself.

   "You have two minutes to write your lifetime goals, starting now."

4. At the end of two minutes, call time. Tell them to take another two minutes to read over what they wrote, make any changes they want, and put their lifetime goals in order of priority. (1 = most important, 2 = next most important, and so on.)

5. When time is up, have them complete this part of the activity by writing down the purpose of the goal that was the highest on their list of priorities. Give them one minute to complete their purpose statement. Examples:

**Goal 1:** To get married and have a family.

**Purpose:** To share love and closeness, and to raise children who will grow up to make a contribution to the world.

**Goal 1:** To become a doctor with a successful practice.

**Purpose:** To help people and to live comfortably.

6. Ask them to turn to the second page of the worksheet.

7. Proceed with these instructions:

- "Next write your five-year goals. These are the things you want to accomplish in the next five years. Consider the same categories as you did with the lifetime goals. Also include goals you have related to school. You have two minutes to make your list.
- "Your time is up. Now, take two more minutes to review what you wrote, make changes, and put your five-year goals in order of priority.
- "Finish this part of the activity by writing a purpose statement for your number 1 goal. You have one minute.
- "Next, turn to the third page of your worksheet. Repeat the process for your six-month goals. Consider the same categories. Again you will have two minutes to make your list.
- "Then spend two more minutes revising and ranking your list of six-month goals.
- "Finally, write the purpose of your number 1 six-month goal.
- "Now turn to the last page of the worksheet. Write your one-month goals. You have two minutes to come up with your list.
- "Then take two more minutes to review and rank your list.
- "To complete the one-month goals, write a statement of purpose for your number 1 goal."

8. After the activity, bring the class together to share about the process. Suggested discussion questions follow:

- "Look at the goals you wrote. How were your one-month goals different from your lifetime goals?"

- "What did you discover about your number 1 goal as you moved from long-term to short-term goals?"
- "What is the connection between your number 1 lifetime goal and your number 1 one-month goal?"
- "Imagine that the path of your life is marked out with goal spaces like a game board. Is your number 1 short-term goal the next step on the path toward achieving your lifetime goal?"
- "If not, consider whether there is another short-term goal that is really number 1, or whether there is a different lifetime goal that is more important to you than the one you identified as number 1."

# LONG TERM, SHORT TERM WORKSHEET

## LIFETIME GOALS

_____

_____

_____

_____

## REVISIONS

_____

_____

_____

_____

Goal 1 _____

Goal 2 _____

Goal 3 _____

## Purpose of Goal 1

_____

_____

## FIVE-YEAR GOALS

_____

_____

_____

_____

## REVISIONS

_____

_____

Goal 1 _____

Goal 2 _____

Goal 3 _____

## Purpose of Goal 1

_____

_____

_____

_____

## SIX-MONTH GOALS

_____

_____

_____

_____

## REVISIONS

_____

_____

Goal 1 _____

Goal 2 _____

Goal 3 _____

## Purpose of Goal 1

_____

_____

_____

_____

## ONE-MONTH GOALS

_____

_____

_____

_____

## REVISIONS

_____

_____

Goal 1 _____

Goal 2 _____

Goal 3 _____

## Purpose of Goal 1

_____

_____

_____

_____

## 66

# *Five-Year Résumé*

## Purpose

This activity can promote student success by helping students be specific about what they would like to accomplish during the next five years.

## Procedure

1. Introduce the activity by saying:

    "Some day in the not-too-distant future when you go to apply for a full-time job, you may need to prepare a form called a résumé. Adult job-seekers often spend lots of time and money writing their résumés. There are even people you can hire to prepare your résumé for you. Sometimes people have their résumés typeset on expensive paper so that they will stand out when potential employers are reading them.

    "On their résumés, people summarize all the things they have done in their education and their past jobs. They make sure to include all their achievements and talents so as to impress the person who might hire them.

    "Today, you are going to write a résumé for yourself. However, yours will be a special kind of résumé, because the achievements you are going to list may not have happened yet."

2. Be sure each student has a pencil and a copy of the Five-Year Résumé Worksheet.

3. Continue by giving the following instructions:

    • "The résumé you are going to write is one that will be true about you *five years from now*. What will the date be five years from today? How old will you be?"

- "From the perspective of five years from now, answer the following questions about yourself. Even though the events may not have occurred yet, put down what you want to be true and have reason to believe you will accomplish between now and five years from now.
  —Name.
  —Address.
  —Phone.
  —Type of job for which you are applying.
  —How many years of education have you completed?
  —Where did you get your high school diploma?
  —Have you had any college experience?
  —If yes, give details.
  —What jobs have you held? List names and addresses of employers, how long you worked, and what your job was.
  —List any extracurricular activities or clubs you participated in, offices held, academic awards, or other honors you earned in high school.
  —List any special talents and skills you have.
  —List people who can be contacted as references to answer questions about your character, talents, and experience. These should be adults who have known you for some time. They could include former employers, family friends, neighbors, former teachers, and so on."

4.  Tell students to go ahead and fill out their résumé worksheet as they want it to be five years from now.

5.  When they are finished, have them find partners. Tell them they are going to role-play going to a job interview. One partner will be the employer, who will ask questions about the other's résumé. Tell them they have about five minutes and then you will tell them to switch roles. Ask them not to switch until you tell them to. You may want to demonstrate this process first by having a student come to the front of the room and role-play with you. You play the part of the employer. (During the exercise, walk around the room and listen in on the students' role-playing. If five minutes seems too long or too short, vary the time accordingly. You may discover that each class is different.)

6.  After five minutes, have them switch roles.

7.  Bring the class together to debrief the process. Here are some possible discussion questions:

- "What did it feel like to have accomplished all the things you wrote on your résumé?"
- "As you were interviewed, did you find the accomplishments becoming more real in your mind?"
- "What accomplishment were you most proud of? Would you like to have that be a *real* accomplishment of yours five years from now?"
- "If that is going to be true five years from now, what steps can you take to make it happen? What can you do in the next 24 hours to take the first step toward making it happen?"

# FIVE-YEAR RÉSUMÉ WORKSHEET

NAME _____

ADDRESS _____

PHONE _____

TYPE OF JOB YOU ARE APPLYING FOR _____

EDUCATIONAL BACKGROUND

|  | Name | Degree | Year Graduated |
|---|---|---|---|
| HIGH SCHOOL | _____ | _____ | _____ |
| COLLEGE | _____ | _____ | _____ |

JOB HISTORY

| Employer | Position | Length of Service |
|---|---|---|
| _____ | _____ | _____ |
| _____ | _____ | _____ |
| _____ | _____ | _____ |

AWARDS AND HONORS EARNED IN HIGH SCHOOL _____

_____

EXTRACURRICULAR ACTIVITIES AND CLUBS _____

_____

SPECIAL TALENTS AND SKILLS _____

_____

CHARACTER REFERENCES

_____

_____

_____

FEIFFER COPYRIGHT 1988 Jules Feiffer. Reprinted with permission of Universal Press Syndicate. All rights reserved.

# 67

# Give It Your Best Shot

> *It is necessary to try to surpass one's self always; this occupation ought to last as long as life.*
>
> —Queen Christina of Sweden

## Purpose

This activity gives students practice in setting goals and reaching them. The object of this game, unlike most games, is not necessarily to score the most points, but to set realistic goals and achieve them. Athletic talent is not so important here as a good knowledge of one's abilities and a willingness to take a moderate risk. In other words, know what's possible, dream a little, and then go for it.

## Materials Needed

- four waste baskets
- four to twelve tennis balls (used tennis balls can usually be obtained free from a country club or tennis club)
- masking tape
- measuring tape or a ruler

## *Procedure*

1. Form four teams of equal size within the class.

2. Have each team select a captain, a coach, and a score keeper. The captain's job will be to cheer people on and urge them to go for it. The coach's job will be to keep everyone in touch with the reality of what they can do. And the score keeper will record each person's distance and points.

3. Supply each team with a waste basket and three tennis balls. The object of the game is to score the most points by getting the ball in the basket from the greatest distance possible, with as much accuracy as possible.

   If a student makes a basket from the first marker (a piece of masking tape 3 feet from the basket), he or she scores 5 points; the second marker (5 feet from the basket), 10 points; and the third marker (10 feet from the basket), 15 points. Before shooting, each student is to set a goal for how many points he or she intends to score.

4. On the first round, students will be practicing to see how skillful they are. They may take three shots from any distance. Using the results of this first round, they are to set a goal for the second round.

5. Before they start the second round, they are to state their goals: how many points they intend to score. The coach encourages them to be realistic, while the team captain challenges them to better their score on the first round.

6. After everyone has had a turn, have them pull their chairs together into a group and discuss what they learned about goal setting. Ask them to consider:

   - "What advice would you give to other players about how to score the maximum number of points?"
   - "How well did you do in achieving your goal?"
   - "If you made your goal, congratulate yourself."
   - "Do you think you could have scored even more points if you had taken a little more risk?"
   - "If you did not make your goal, what happened? Did you set your goal too high?"
   - "If the way you performed in this activity were an example of the way you relate to all your goals, what conclusions could you draw?"

*The* difference between a successful person and others is not a lack of strength, not a lack of knowledge, but rather a lack of will.

—Vince Lombardi

SPERM BANK

LOOK, LADY — YOU'RE THE ONE WHO ASKED FOR A FAMOUS MOVIE STAR WITH DARK HAIR, STRONG NOSE AND DEEP SET EYES...

# Be SMART About Goals

## Purpose

The purpose of this activity is to have students learn goal-setting guidelines that increase the likelihood of success.

## Procedure

1. Tell your students that they are now going to select one goal from any of the different activities they've done so far on goals. The goals they select should be very important to them, goals they feel they can achieve.

2. Direct them to look at their notes from the previous activities to choose a goal: the "Life Assessment" activity (56); their intentions in the "Secret Number 1: Get Rid of Expectations" activity (59); their goals in "Long Term, Short Term" (65); the achievements they identified in their "Five-Year Résumé" (66).

3. After they have selected the goal they want to work on, have them write it at the top of the worksheet labeled "Be SMART About Goals."

4. Now lead your students through each of five guidelines as follows:

---

The concept of SMART goals appears in somewhat different versions in a number of different references. We are unaware of the original source.

"Suppose you went to McDonald's for some lunch and when the clerk asked what you wanted, you replied, 'Give me something.'

"Is it likely that you would get what you want? Is it possible that you wouldn't get anything at all? What's the matter with your order? If you said that your order isn't stated clearly, congratulations! You just discovered the first clue. S stands for *specific*. When you are writing a goal, be as specific, precise, and exact as possible in describing what you want."

**Too General:**     "I want to be successful."

**Specific:**          "My goal is to graduate high school and go on to college."

"**S** stands for *SPECIFIC*."

5. Ask the students to reread the goals they wrote at the top of their papers. Are they specific? If not, have them rewrite the goals now to make them as specific as possible.

    **Coaching Questions**
    - "Exactly what are you saying that you want?"
    - "Precisely what do you mean?"
    - "When you have accomplished this goal, what will it look like or feel like?"

6. Continue the discussion with the students: "What's the matter with this goal: 'My goal is to lose weight'?

    "If you said there's no way to tell whether the goal has been reached, congratulations. You've just discovered the second clue. M stands for *measurable*. You must know where you were when you started and where you are when you finish, in order to know whether you reached your goal."

    **Too General:**     "My goal is to lose weight."

    **Measurable:**     "My goal is to lose fifteen pounds."

    "**M** stands for *measurable*."

7. Have students look again at their goals. Is each goal measurable? If not, have them rewrite so that each goal has a built-in system for measuring progress.

### Coaching Questions

- "How will you know when you have accomplished your goal?"
- "How much will you weigh?"
- "On a scale of 1–10, where are you now? On the same scale, where will you be when you've achieved your goal?"

8.  The discussion continues: "Into McDonald's again. There is a new order clerk. This time you're in a fanciful mood. You order a diamond-studded hamburger on a solid gold bun!

    "Did you figure out what's the matter with your order? McDonald's doesn't have solid gold buns? Right. Even the most determined goal seeker can't attain goals that aren't achievable.

    "**A** stands for *achievable*."

    "What about your goal? Is it actually achievable? If not, get real and rewrite your goal."

### Coaching Questions

- "Is that realistic?"
- "How do you *know* it can be done?"
- "What skills and talents will you need to achieve this?"

9.  Moving on to the next guideline: "Your goal is to become a teacher because your mother thinks it would be a good job for you.

    "What's the matter with that? You say, you don't want to do it? Let your mother become a teacher herself? Correct. The next clue is *responsible*—are you willing to be responsible for it? Is it something you desire?

    "Look again at your goal. Is it something you really want for yourself? Or is it something you think you should want, something your mother or father or teacher wants you to have? If your goal isn't something you actually want, you won't be motivated to achieve it. So change it to something that is going to truly satisfy you.

    "**R** in SMART stands for *responsible*, meaning that you own it, it is something you personally desire."

### Coaching Questions

- "What about this goal interests you?"

- "What benefit will you gain from accomplishing it?"
- "What is your purpose for achieving it?"

10. "You've decided that your sister has been sneaking into McDonald's too often when you're not around, and she's getting fat! You have a goal for her to go on a diet and lose 10 pounds.

   "What's the matter with this goal? Oh, you say you can't lose weight for somebody else? Congratulations, you've solved the other part of this clue.

   "Responsible also means that it is within *your* control. Look at your goal again to check if your goal is something you can control."

### Coaching Questions

- "Are you in a position to bring this about?"
- "Is it dependent on anyone else? If so, how can you guarantee that the other person will do his or her part?"
- "How can you state it so that you can be *completely* responsible for accomplishing what you intend?"

11. "The final point has to do with time. "What if you had a goal to 'get a mini-bike someday'? Is anything the matter with that goal?

   "If you noticed that the word *someday* is so vague that you might not get your bike until you're 85, clever you! You're onto clue number 5.

**"T** stands for *time frame*."

"Check your goal and indicate by when you intend to accomplish it."

### Coaching Questions

- "When or by when will you have achieved it?"
- "In order to accomplish your goal within the time frame, what steps will you have to take, and by when does each need to be completed?"
- "Where will you find the time to do what's necessary for this goal? Will there be other things you won't be able to do?"

12. After completing the worksheet, give your students an opportunity to share their revised goals in pairs, small groups, or with the entire class.

# BE SMART ABOUT GOALS WORKSHEET

## GOAL

_____

_____

Specific—What specifically do you intend to achieve?

_____

_____

Measurable—How will you know when you've achieved it?

_____

_____

Achievable—Is it realistic?

_____

_____

Responsible—Are you willing to be responsible for it? Is it desirable? Are you able to be responsible for it? Is it controllable?

_____

_____

Time frame—By when will you have accomplished it?

_____

_____

# Goal Line

## Purpose

This activity can encourage your students to take action on their goals and to keep track of their accomplishments.

## Materials Needed

For this activity, you will need to make a large bulletin board on which to display the students' goal markers. Make the bulletin board look like a football or soccer field with an end zone at the bottom for the starting line and another at the top for the goal line. Divide the field into 10-yard marks to make 100 yards.

Have students make their goal markers and pin or staple them at the starting line. Each day that students meet their goals, the markers are advanced 20 yards toward the goal line. Their goal markers may be index cards with their names on, cut in the shape of footballs, have photographs of the students, or cut in shapes unique and special to each student.

## Procedure

1.  Introduce the activity to your class as follows:

    "Did you ever wonder why they call it the goal line? It's because the goal line is where you score points. If you want to score points in achieving your goals, you have to keep track of what your goals are, and how close you are to the goal line with each of them. Today you'll be starting a week-long activity designed to help you keep track of your goals and monitor your progress every day."

2. Give the following instructions:

   - "Look at the goal you have been working with in the previous activities. What could you accomplish during the next week that would move you forward toward your goal?
   - "Think of how to state a one-week goal, remembering to be SMART." (You may want to review the SMART guidelines with them at this point. "Who remembers what S stands for?" and so on.)
   - "On your goal marker, draw a symbol that represents your goal. It could be a picture of a report card, musical instrument, or a scale if your goal is to lose weight and so on.
   - "Print the one-week goal neatly inside the symbol you have drawn. Sign your name under your goal.
   - "Now put that card to one side, and take a second card.
   - "What could you complete during the next 24 hours that would move you toward the one-week goal? On the second card write a 24-hour goal related to your one-week goal."

3. When their two cards are completed, have them pull their chairs into a class circle. Let them take turns reading their one-week goals and their 24-hour goals to the class.

4. After they have read their goals, have each student go to the bulletin board and post the card with the symbol and one-week goal at the starting line.

5. Have them keep the 24-hour goal cards with them to remind them what to do.

6. Each day for a week, have the students report on their success with the 24-hour goals. They are to move their markers 20 yards for each day they are successful.

7. If certain students are not succeeding, you may want to provide them with support in identifying what is going on. Do this in a nonjudgmental manner, looking to discover the facts of the situation.

   Perhaps the goal was unrealistic and needs to be modified, or maybe aspects of it are beyond the student's control. The questions provided on the "Goals Update" page in Chapter Seven should prove useful to you in coaching students on their goals.

8.   If some students are coming in with excuses of not completing their goals, the next two activities will help you address these.

9.   When a student gets to the goal line, plan some sort of acknowledgment or celebration such as a standing ovation from the class, a small prize, a note home, or whatever you feel will work best with your students.

# Yeah, But . . .

> *I*'m not afraid of storms, for I'm learning how to sail my ship.
>
> —Jo in Louisa May Alcott's *Little Women*

## Purpose

This activity helps students anticipate possible obstacles to their success so that they can be more proactive in dealing with these obstacles effectively.

When people think about setting goals for themselves, what often comes up is a series of obstacles to success . . . the YEAH, BUTS. You probably have heard them before:

"YEAH, I'd like to get good grades, BUT I don't have time to study."
"YEAH, I'd like to be on the team, BUT I'm too small."
"YEAH, I'd like to be popular, BUT I'm not good looking enough."
"YEAH, I'd like to go to college, BUT my folks don't have the money."

The YEAH, BUT excuse functions like an escape hatch. We say we want to accomplish a goal, but we have a built-in excuse for not being successful or for not even making the effort in the first place.

The interesting thing is that when we really, *really* want to accomplish something, we find ways to do it. All the YEAH, BUTS in the world don't matter a bit then.

Here's a chance for your students to discover how much they really want to achieve their goals, or whether they are going to let the YEAH, BUTS get in their way.

## Procedure

1. Distribute YEAH, BUT Worksheet.

2. Tell each student to find a partner, and then give these directions:

   - "You are going to interview your partner to find out what blocks might get in the way of accomplishing his or her goal. Start by writing the goal at the top of the sheet (in the end zone)."
   - "Now say to your partner, 'Your goal is to _____ _____, but what could get in your way?' Keep asking this or similar questions, probing until you fill in all 10 blanks on the sheet."

     **A:** "Your goal is to get an *A* in math, but what could get in your way?"

     **B:** "Well, if I don't study harder, I could flunk the next test."

     **A:** "Your goal is to get an *A* in math, but what could get in your way?"

     **B:** "My belief that I'm not good in math."

     **A:** "Your goal is to get an *A* in math, but what could get in your way?"

     **B:** "My feeling that I would rather be playing than studying."

   - "Change places, and let your partner ask you about your goal. When you finish, get your own sheet back, so you can see what you are up against."

3. After the interviews are finished, have the students pull their chairs into a class circle. Go around the group asking students to identify YEAH, BUTS that could keep them from achieving their goals.

   As they listen to other people talk, ask them to decide whether it sounds as though their goals or their YEAH, BUTS are more likely to win out. How can they tell?

4. Complete the activity with a discussion:

   - "What did you learn by doing this process?"

- "Does it seem right now that the goal you set is something you really want?"
- "Are you willing to do whatever it takes to get it, including going through the blocks in your way?"
- "Were some of the YEAH, BUTS obvious excuses, not real obstacles?"
- "Were others serious enough that they could still block you from reaching your goal?"

## Follow-Up Activity

1. Have students list any of the YEAH, BUT statements that seem serious enough to possibly keep them from achieving their goals.

2. For each block, have them list the resources they have—both strengths within themselves and help from other people—that they can use to overcome the blocks.

> *Obstacles are those frightful things you see when you take your eyes off your goals.*
>
> —Anonymous

Stated Goal

Yeah Buts

# 71

## *Favorite Excuses*

> *T*he guy who usually tells you about the football
> taking crazy bounces is the guy who dropped it.
>
> —Lou Holtz, college football coach

## Purpose

This activity helps students to realize that they can either have what they want in life (their goals), or they can have the excuses for why they don't have what they want.

"The dog ate my homework."
"The car broke down."
"My mother didn't wake me up in time."
"Somebody stole my pencil."
"Nobody told me!"

Do you recognize these? They are famous favorite excuses that every kid learns along with the *ABC*s. Everybody has a sackful of excuses, good for any occasion. What's your excuse? (And don't try to use the excuse that you couldn't think of an excuse!)

## Materials Needed

- Post-it® pads

## Procedure

1. Have the students bring their chairs into a class circle.

2. Give them each a stack of Post-it notes.

3. Tell them that they are going to be writing excuses on the Post-it notes, one excuse per note.

4. Instruct them as follows:

   - "First write all the excuses you can think of for not getting your homework done. Remember, one excuse per note."
   - "Next, write all the excuses you know for not getting to school on time."
   - "Now all the excuses for not taking out the garbage."
   - "Now all the ones for not cleaning your room."
   - "All the excuses you have for not liking yourself."
   - "All the excuses you have for others not liking you."
   - "All the excuses for not doing well in school."
   - "All the excuses for not finishing your 24-hour goal."

5. Go around the circle and have students read off their favorite excuses and post them on a "Favorite Excuses" bulletin board.

6. You may want to explore with your students what motivates people to settle for the excuse rather than succeed at a goal. What purpose does excuse-making serve?

   Sometimes excuses are ways we have of protecting ourselves. We protect ourselves from the discomfort of feeling like a failure if we have a good excuse for not having met our goal. We can avoid the fear of punishment if we can convince our parents that we had a good enough reason for not doing what we were told. We can save face with our friends if we can blame our parents for not letting us stay out all night.

7. In the future, when a student gives an excuse for something, you can simply point to the "Favorite Excuses" bulletin board and suggest that it is not necessary to make up a new one—that we already have plenty to pick from. Remind them that **you can have what you want (your goal) or you can have the excuses why you don't.**

DENNIS THE MENACE® used by permission of Hank Ketcham and © 1991 by North America Syndicate

*F*ar away there in the sunshine are my highest aspirations. I may not reach them, but I can look up and see their beauty, believe in them and try to follow where they lead.

—Louisa May Alcott

# 72

# Affirmations

> **A**s a man thinketh in his heart, so is he.
>
> —Proverbs 23:7

## Purposes

This activity has five purposes:

- to empower students to overcome negative attitudes and learning blocks
- to develop greater self-esteem in students
- to teach students how to program themselves for success
- to teach students to strive for goals and dreams on a daily basis
- to create several personal and class affirmations that will support the students academically, socially, and personally.

Affirmations are positive statements that affirm or declare a desired objective as if it were already achieved. The purpose of the affirmation is to create "structural tension" in the brain, which thereby creates the internal motivation to take the necessary actions required to achieve the goal. This structural tension can be further increased by using the affirmation in conjunction with a clear visual image of the desired outcome.

87

Whenever the mind simultaneously holds two realities that do not match, "cognitive dissonance" or "structural tension" arises. The process looks like this:

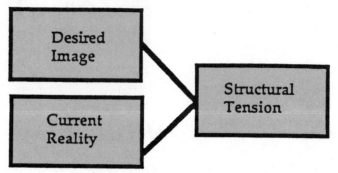

If your current reality is that you are a C student and you affirm and visualize being an A student, then you will experience structural tension. If you deliberately create and hold this structural tension in your mind on a daily basis, it will intensify and create the following mental changes:

1. You will begin to experience creative ideas that will help you achieve your goal.
2. You will start to perceive all kinds of internal and external resources to help you achieve your goal that you were never aware of before. Your awareness will expand to take in new data to help you.
3. You will experience increasing motivation to take action.

We can diagram it as follows:

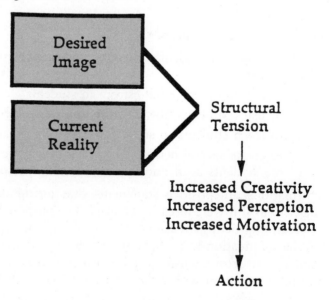

All motivation comes from having a picture of something you want that does not match the picture of what you have. The more you can increase the interplay between those two images, the more you will increase your motivation. Affirmations, which are word pictures describing the completed goal, help elicit visual pictures, thus increasing the structural tension and motivation.

The beliefs, expectations, and thought patterns that your students currently hold also determine their self-esteem, and how willing they are to participate in school and in life. If students believe that they are slow learners, C-students, not mathematically inclined, physically awkward, or stupid, then that is what they will create. The belief and the picture will create the future and will control their actions.

Precisely because they are constantly controlled by their beliefs, students can learn to override their self-defeating beliefs through the use of affirmations and transform their internal experience of themselves, and they will also gradually modify their daily behavior to match their new beliefs.

## Procedures

Developing personal and classroom affirmations takes approximately a week, depending on the number of affirmations per student and how elaborate you want to make them.

### Step One

Ask the students to refer to their goal lists and to select at least three goals they have that they wish to accomplish by the time they become adults (or graduate from high school). Have them be as concrete and as specific as possible. In their support groups, instruct students to discuss in detail their goals and describe what their lives will be like once they have obtained their goals.

### Step Two

Have the students identify at least 10 strengths they possess that will help them reach their goals. Be adamant in requiring that every student list at least 10 strengths: for example, determination, humor, sensitivity, guts, enthusiasm, a positive go-for-it attitude, and commitment. Make sure they state the qualities in a sensitive manner. For example, "stubbornness" would be written as "perseverance." (See the facing page for a list of strengths. You may wish to reproduce this list as a resource for the students.)

able to give orders
able to take care of self
able to take orders
accept advice
admire others
affectionate
alive
appreciative
articulate
artistic
assertive
athletic
attractive

brave
bright
businesslike

calm
can be firm if necessary
caring
clean
committed
common sense
communicates well
compassionate
considerate
cooperative
courteous
creative

daring
dedicated
dependable
diligent
disciplined
do what needs to be done
don't give up

eager to please
effective
efficient
elegant
encourage others
enjoy taking care of others

fair
feeling forceful
frank and honest
friendly

generous
get along with others
get things done
give a lot
goal setter
good cook
good dancer
good friend
good leader
good listener
good looking
good manners
good neighbor
good parent
good singer
good with details
good with words
good with my hands
graceful
grateful

happy
hard worker
healthy
helpful
honest
humorous

independent
inspiring
intelligent

joyful

keep agreements
kind and reassuring

leadership
like responsibility
lots of friends
lovable
loving
loyal

make a difference
make a good impression
mathematical
mechanical
motivate others
musical

never give up

observant
often admired
on time
orderly
organized
open

patient
peaceful
physically fit
pleasant
positive in attitude

quick learner

religious
resilient
respected by others
respectful of authority
responsible
risk taker

self-confident
self-reliant
self-respecting
sense of humor
sensitive
speak several languages
spiritual
spontaneous
stand up for myself
straightforward and direct
strong

team player
tolerant
trusting
truthful

understanding
unselfish

visionary

warm
well-dressed

Have students explain how each quality will help them reach their goals. Identifying strengths in light of accomplishing goals is an excellent method of sensitizing students to their positive qualities.

## Step Three

Now your students have two lists: goals and strengths. From these lists, they will develop their affirmations. Instruct the students to make an affirmation for every goal that they have. Remind them to incorporate their strengths as they make their affirmations. See the later section entitled "How to Create Affirmations" for more detailed instructions on how to elicit affirmations from students.

To get maximum value from an affirmation, adhere as closely as possible to the following guidelines.

## Guidelines for Affirmations

1. Be personal. Start with the words "I am . . ." Affirmations for the whole class begin "We are . . ."

2. Use present tense. Describe what you want as though you already have it or it is already accomplished.

   No:  "I am getting a red Peugeot bicycle."
   Yes:  "I am enjoying riding my red Peugeot bicycle."

3. Describe it in positive terms.

   No:  "I am getting rid of my fear of flying."
   Yes:  "I am enjoying the thrill of flying."

4. Be brief.

5. Be specific. Vague affirmations produce vague results. (Remember the *S* in setting SMART goals.)

6. Include an action word ending with "-ing."

   No:  "I express myself openly, honestly, and with exhilaration."
   Yes:  "I am exhilarated, *expressing* myself openly and honestly."

7. Include at least one dynamic feeling word, such as "enjoying," "adoring," "thrilled," "excited," "exhilarated," "peacefully," or "feeling great."

91

> **No:** "I am living at my perfect weight."
> "I am expressing my true feelings."
>
> **Yes:** "I am looking and feeling great at my perfect weight."
> "I am enjoying expressing my true feelings with comfort and ease."

8. Change yourself, not the other person.

> **No:** "Everyone is treating me with respect."
> **Yes:** "I am self-confident and calm as I effectively communicate with others."

An affirmation is on target when it is easy to say, and makes the student smile with excitement. Sometimes the excitement may be accompanied by some mild discomfort. That usually means the affirmation is beginning to motivate the student toward new, more self-nurturing and self-expressive actions.

When students have doubts about their affirmations, have them employ this fool-proof quality control technique. Say to them, "Close your eyes, say your affirmation, and then watch what internal picture it evokes. If it is the picture of what you truly want, then those are the appropriate words."

## Step Four

Have students create affirmation cards and decorate them. Affirmation cards can be made out of anything from plain notebook paper and pencil or pen, to construction paper with crayons, markers, and paint. If possible, go all out and have students make affirmation cards from construction paper, markers, and crayons. Encourage them to cut and paste pictures from magazines on their cards to illustrate their affirmations.

Although making affirmation cards may take more than two class periods, it is a very productive, worthwhile activity. Have them work in groups and share materials and ideas.

Affirmation cards should be no smaller than half a piece of notebook paper, and no larger than a full sheet. Ask your students to carry their affirmations in their notebooks at all times, so that they may refer to them throughout the day.

## Step Five

Students take out their affirmation cards and say them out loud at the beginning of every class.

## Step Six (optional)

Ask each buddy group to create an affirmation for themselves as a group. The affirmation must reflect a common goal of everyone in the group. This could be anything from a shared personal desire to a shared educational goal. Once the group unanimously agrees on an affirmation, everyone participates in creating and decorating the group's affirmation card. Use full-size construction paper or poster board. Display the affirmation cards of each group on a bulletin board in the classroom.

Students say their group's affirmation at the beginning of each class just before their personal affirmations.

## Step Seven (optional)

Ask the class as a whole to make up an affirmation or two that reflect the way they wish the class to function. One class affirmation was, "We are enjoying learning and growing in honors English." These same students also created an individual affirmation that was more personal and reflected how they wished to perform in the class: "I am enjoying honors English and easily getting an A." Have them say these affirmations in unison at the beginning of each day before they do their group and personal affirmations.

## *How to Create Affirmations*

1.  Ask the students to visualize what they would like to create. Ask them to see the result they want to create or the way they want things to be. Ask them to place themselves inside their pictures and see the scene as if they were looking through their own eyes. If they want a certain kind of bicycle, for example, they should see the world as they would if they were riding such a bicycle.

2.  Ask them to hear the sounds they would hear if everything were happening the way they wanted it to be. In the case of the bicycle, they would hear the road noises, the sounds of friends riding with them, and the voices of people congratulating them for having such a fine bike.

3.  Ask them to experience the feelings they think they would feel if this goal were already realized.

4.  Ask them to describe in a brief statement what they would be experiencing, including what they would be feeling, as if they were describing it to someone else. For example, "I am happily showing my report card with all 'A's on it to my father," or "I am proudly

accepting the 'Most Valuable Player Award' at the annual sports awards dinner."

5.  Again, edit the affirmations to make them fit the preceding guidelines. Do this with them, or have them break up into small groups to check each others' affirmations.

## Working with Affirmations

Once students have chosen a goal, and created and edited their affirmation to meet the guidelines, there are several ways to work with them. Students may repeat their affirmations silently or aloud. They can say them in unison or write them down. The key to their use is constant repetition over time.

## Silent Repetition

In the silent repetition method, simply ask the students to close their eyes and visualize themselves already doing that which they desire to do (reading easily), having what they want to have (owning a 10-speed bike), or being the way they want to be (relaxed while taking a test). Once they have created a clear image, they are to continue to see the image while repeating their affirmation silently to themselves over and over again for about a minute. The best times for silent repetition are two minutes during the first period of the day, two minutes before lunch, and two minutes at the end of the day.

An example of this form of affirmation would be to have a group of elementary school students close their eyes and visualize themselves reading successfully and easily. They could see themselves reading a new book to one of their parents, or reading out loud in front of the whole class. They would then repeat their affirmation, which might be "I am joyfully reading everything easily and well."

## Group Affirmations

A second method of working with affirmations is to repeat them out loud in unison. Have your students close their eyes and say out loud with you the chosen affirmation. Repeat the affirmation for at least a minute. For example, "Math is easy and fun. . . . Math is easy and fun. . . . Math is easy and fun. . . ." If you or one of your students plays some musical instrument such as a guitar, autoharp, or piano, you can set the affirmation to music and sing it over and over. This is very effective.

## The All-Purpose Antidote Affirmation

One group affirmation we recommend that you use with all your classes is,

**"N**o matter what you say or do to me, I'm still a worthwhile person."

We recommend that you use this affirmation on a daily basis, much like a one-a-day multiple vitamin tablet for the mind. This will build the internal mental strength to replace all negative input from other people (put-downs and teasing) with a positive affirmation. Have the students repeat the affirmation for a minute. Then say negative things to them such as: "You are ugly," "I hate you," "You are a nerd," "You flunked math," and "You're fired," while they respond, in unison, "No matter what you say or do to me, I'm still a worthwhile person."

## Turnaround Statements

A turnaround statement is simply an affirmation created to counteract a negative belief, chronic negative self-talk, or someone else's judgment or limitation that the student has internalized. You may relate this to the "Yeah But" activity, perhaps even having the students write affirmations to turn around their "Yeah But." Use turnaround or antidote statements when:

1. You discover a limiting belief inside yourself.
2. You catch yourself in negative self-talk.
3. Someone else makes a negative remark about or to you.

To create a turnaround statement:

1. Identify the limiting statement or belief.
2. Determine how it limits you.
3. Decide how you want to be, act, or feel.
4. Create a statement that affirms this.

### Examples

| | |
|---|---|
| **Negative:** | "If I eat this cake, it will go straight to my hips." |
| **Turnaround:** | "No matter what I eat, I am looking and feeling great in my gorgeous, slim body." |

95

| | |
|---|---|
| **Negative:** | "Don't express your feelings. People will think you are weak." |
| **Turnaround:** | "The more I express my feelings, the more people are honestly loving and supporting me." |
| **Negative:** | "You're such a slob! You never pick up after yourself." |
| **Turnaround:** | "I am a neat and organized person," or "I am creative in my organization and decorating." |
| **Negative:** | "I'm stupid." |
| **Turnaround:** | "I'm smart." |

## Seed Planting

Another method for working with affirmations is called "seed planting," since what we are doing is planting a new seed in the student's thoughts. Good seeds to plant are affirmations or turnaround statements.

The student who is to receive the seed planting sits in the middle of the class and closes his or her eyes (let's say *her,* for this example). She says her affirmation three times out loud, with great gusto and enthusiasm. Then the rest of the students face her and repeat her personal affirmation over and over again until she raises her hand to signify that she has fully taken it in. Advise the student in the middle to take as long as she needs. The affirmation should begin with the person's first name, as in the following example: "Nancy, you are creative and smart . . ."

## Tape Recorders

A variation on seed planting is to encourage students with tape recorders to record their affirmations, and then play them back to themselves twice a day, each morning just after awaking, and each night before falling asleep. A few students with whom we have worked decided to have their parents record their affirmations onto the tape. They reported that it was a very effective technique. For students whose parents do not want to do so, you may record the affirmation. Just having an adult voice repeatedly validating a positive behavior or state of being can be very nurturing for a child.

## Affirmation Art

Have the students create posters or collages illustrating their affirmations. Make sure their affirmation is printed on the poster somewhere. This process brings in the visual dimension quite strongly, and encourages them to interact with the image they want. They can hang up their posters in the classroom or at home. The best places to hang them are on the bedroom or bathroom mirror, the refrigerator door, or anywhere else they will be seen frequently.

## Writing Affirmations

Another effective method for working with affirmations is the written approach. Have your students write their affirmations 10 times each on a sheet of paper in the first person, present tense. Some educators suggest that the students use their first name in the affirmation as follows: "I, Jack, am calmly remembering everything I need and want to remember."

If your students also write their affirmations in the second and third person, then the effect can be even more impactful: "You, Jack, are remembering everything you need and want to remember," and "He, Jack, is remembering everything he needs and wants to remember."

The rationale behind using all three persons is that we form our unconscious beliefs about ourselves and our abilities from what we say to ourselves about ourselves (first person), what others say to us (second person), and what we hear or overhear others say about us (third person). Therefore, when using the written method you may wish to have your students write their affirmations 10 times daily in the first, second, and third persons until their affirmation becomes reality. At that point they may choose another affirmation with which to work.

| | | |
|---|---|---|
| adorable | fun-loving | overjoyed |
| adoring | fulfilled | peaceful |
| beautiful | gentle | pleasant |
| blissful | glad | pleased |
| calm | gorgeous | quiet |
| celebrating | grateful | rapturous |
| centered | gratified | ravishing |
| cheerful | great | rejoicing |
| confident | handsome | relaxed |
| content | happy | relishing |
| delighted | hilarious | revelling |
| easily | jolly | satisfied |
| ecstatic | joyous | serene |
| elegant | jubilant | soaring |
| enchanted | lively | stunning |
| enjoying | lovely | tender |
| enthusiastic | loving | thrilled |
| excellent | merry | tranquil |
| excited | mirthful | triumphant |
| exhilarated | outrageous | wonderful |

*Note:* Most words can also be used with "-ly" added. For example, you could also use *joyfully, calmly,* and *merrily.*

# Reaction Column Affirmations

When using the written method, you may also want to have the students use the Reaction Column Technique. Have them divide a page in half lengthwise. Direct them to write affirmations on the left-hand side of the page. On the right-hand side, they are to write any negative thoughts or reactions that come up as they are writing their affirmations and create turnaround statements to counteract the negative responses.

### Student Example

**Affirmation**

"I am remembering everything I need or want to remember."

**Reaction**

"You forgot five things in yesterday's history lesson."

**Turnaround/New Affirmation**

"I am easily remembering everything I study in history class."

### Teacher Example

**Affirmation**

"I am teaching perfectly every day."

**Reaction**

"It's impossible to teach well with all the discipline problems I've got!"

### Modified Affirmation

"I am easily, lovingly, and effectively teaching my best every day."

### Reaction

"You get upset when Billy starts acting up. And it's impossible some days to be loving toward Judy. Certain kids just aren't easy to love, no matter how hard you try. And being loving doesn't always help them understand the lesson."

### Turnaround

"The more I am loving, the easier it is for me to teach effectively, and the easier it is for me to love every student more."

After the students have completed writing their affirmations and recording their reactions, have them go back and write an "antidote statement" for each of their negative reactions. The following page contains a more detailed explanation suitable for handing out to students.

## AFFIRM, REACT, REAFFIRM

When you work with an affirmation, one effect will be to bring to the surface any beliefs, attitudes, thoughts, or judgments that have kept you from having what you want. If you affirm good grades, every belief you have about how impossible it is for you to make good grades will come up as a reason to stop using the affirmation. (When these negative beliefs arise, this is one sign that the affirmation is working.)

When this happens, you have two choices. One is to continue working with the affirmation and work right through the negative beliefs, attitudes, and thoughts. Another approach is to spend some time identifying the particular beliefs that are surfacing and to modify your affirmation or create new ones to deal with these beliefs. The reaction column affirmation technique is designed to help you create new affirmations to overcome these limiting beliefs.

## Instructions

1. "Divide a sheet of paper into two columns, headed 'Affirmation' and 'Reaction.'

2. "Write out your affirmation, using your name. ('I, Fred, am joyfully receiving all the love I deserve.')

3. "Stop, take a breath, and note any reactive thoughts in the 'Reaction' column.

4. "Repeat this four more times.

5. "Write the affirmations five times in the second person, pausing each time to write any responses. ('You, Fred, are joyfully receiving all the love you deserve.')

6. "Repeat five times in the third person. ('He, Fred, is joyfully receiving all the love he deserves.')

7. "Go over the responses. Some will feel dull, while others will feel charged with energy. Go over the 'charged' ones, and either incorporate the new information into the affirmation, or create a new affirmation, or turnaround statement.

8. "Work with your affirmation until all the reactions are neutralized or positive. At this point, you will have dealt with all your blocks and be able to create more powerfully with this affirmation."

## Some Reminders

Affirmations work best in conjunction with positive visual imagery. Underscore for the students the importance of visualizing the desired outcome of each affirmation and of letting themselves feel as deeply as possible the emotions they would feel when the desired result has actually occurred. Creating the feelings to accompany the image is crucial to the effectiveness of this technique.

Remind the students that when they create or use affirmations, they are to avoid the future tense. Tell the students to always phrase their affirmations in the present tense as if the result already exists. Do not say, "I will become a better reader," but rather "I am reading everything easily and well." Although some people think that this is self-delusion or lying, it isn't. This technique simply acknowledges that everything we create manifests first in our minds before it becomes objective reality.

Affirmations should always be phrased in the most positive way possible. The reason is that negative phrasing evokes negative images, which the subconscious does not know how to turn around into a positive image. Therefore, have your students affirm what they do want rather than what they don't want. Instead of "I no longer have trouble doing math," have them say, "I am now doing math easily and well." This will ensure the most positive results.

A general rule is to keep affirmations short and to the point. They should be strong statements that convey strong feeling tones. The stronger the feeling tone, the more effective the result.

## SAMPLE AFFIRMATIONS

To get you started, we have listed some sample affirmations, which fall into three categories: "Self-Esteem and Responsibility," "Learning," and "For the Teacher." The section "For the Teacher" contains affirmations that you can use to foster your own personal growth and professional development.

### *Affirmations for Self-Esteem and Responsibility*

1. "I am enjoying being lovable and capable."
2. "I am feeling great, respecting myself as a worthwhile, valuable, and important person."
3. "I am a powerful being, radiating my light and love."
4. "I am respecting my own uniqueness and joyfully expressing who I am."
5. "I am easily expressing my ideas freely and joyfully accepting the respect of others."
6. "I am happily loving myself fully just the way I am."
7. "I am enjoying being kind, compassionate, and gentle with myself and others."
8. "I am enjoying the sense of power that comes from being responsible for my life."
9. "I am surprisingly pleased at how powerful I am."
10. "I, _____, am peacefully liking myself more and more each day."
11. "I, _____, am enthusiastically taking responsibility for my life."
12. "I, _____, am confidently asking for what I want."

13. "I, _____, am calmly trusting myself and going at my own speed."

14. "I, _____, am proudly experiencing total success in all I do (in school, in math, in science, in sports, in dating, and so on)."

15. "I, _____, am successful, confidently pursuing all my dreams."

16. "I am proudly being responsible for my own actions."

17. "I am knowingly being responsible for making my relationship with my parents work."

18. "I am effectively keeping my agreements and recognizing the power of my word."

19. "I am effortlessly in touch with my 'inner wisdom' and experience being successful in solving my own problems."

20. "I am enjoying setting and achieving SMART goals."

21. "I am enjoying being nice to my classmates and teacher."

22. "I am peacefully accepting that no matter what you say or do to me, I am still a worthwhile person."

23. "I am serenely and easily accepting compliments, and joyously sharing my successes with others."

24. "I am joyfully accepting and carrying out all my responsibilities."

## Affirmations for Learning

1. "I, _____, am learning math easily and well." (Use any subject.)

2. "I, _____, am happily expressing confidence in my ability to learn."

3. "I, _____, am easily remembering all I see and hear."

4. "I, _____, am learning math more easily and quickly every day."

5. "Reading is easy and fun!" (Use any subject or behavior.)

6. "I, _____, am scoring well on all my tests."

7. "I, _____, am experiencing myself as relaxed and alert."

8. "I am happily remembering that everyone in this class is here to help me learn."

9. "I am confidently feeling free to talk and participate in class."

10. "I am enthusiastically expressing myself."

11. "I am easily expressing my ability to put my feelings into words."

12. "I am finding it easier and easier to do my homework."

13. "I am joyfully doing all my homework and celebrating my good grades."

14. "I am calmly learning more and more each and every day."

15. "I, _____, am (verb)_____ing faster every day."

16. "I am enjoying coming in quietly and getting ready for work."

17. "I am consistently enjoying doing my best work."

## Affirmations for You, the Teacher

1. "I, _____, am truly enjoying myself and have a renewed sense of enthusiasm for teaching."

2. "I, _____, am enthusiastically enjoying learning and practicing new ways to teach."

3. "I, _____, am responsibly modeling for my students the qualities of _____ and _____ whom I admire."

4. "I, _____, am joyfully fulfilling my true purpose and realizing my vision as an educator."

5. "I, _____, am powerfully realizing myself as the source of my experience and the creator of my reality."

6. "I am successfully achieving SMART goals in all areas of my life."

7. "I am competently using all my coaching skills to empower students."

8. "I, _____, am easily loving and supporting my students to be all they can be."

9. "I, _____, am easily responding to every classroom situation, accepting whatever happens as part of the learning process."

10. "I am constantly using all the resources, energy, and time that I need to encourage student happiness and success."

11. "I am feeling relaxed, calm, and at peace with myself."

12. "I am a complete and perfect being, calmly accepting myself just the way I am."

13. "I am consciously loving and fostering the spirit of love and community in my students."

14. "I am effortlessly in touch with my 'inner wisdom' and I'm being with my students in a way that contributes significantly to their lives."

15. "I am easily adapting all the activities in this book to my teaching."

If you or any of your students have any trouble believing that the affirmations will work, use this affirmation:

"I, _____, am trusting that my affirmations are working and that my efforts are paying off."

# MY AFFIRMATIONS

1. _____

_____

2. _____

_____

3. _____

_____

4. _____

_____

5. _____

_____

6. _____

_____

7. _____

_____

8. _____

_____

9. _____

_____

10. _____

_____

# 74

# Report Card

## Purpose

In the last activity, we were discussing "cognitive dissonance" as it relates to affirmations. This exercise works on the same principle applied to student's academic achievement. The purpose is to motivate students to improve their grades.

## Materials Needed

- blank report card forms (14 per student)
- an envelope for each student

## Procedure

1. Give each student 14 blank report card forms.

2. Instruct each student to take one copy of the form and write down all the necessary information: his or her name, classes, teachers, and so on.

3. Then have the students think about what grades they would like to see on their report cards.

   Make the point that the grades don't necessarily have to be straight A's. "Remember, be SMART. If your goal isn't at least within the realm of reason, this cognitive dissonance stuff probably won't work."

4. Tell your students to write in the grades they want to see on their report cards—"the grade you believe you actually are capable of earning at this point."

5. Have them bring their completed report cards with them to share with the entire group.

6. After they have shown their report cards to the class, ask them to agree to repeat this activity—writing out report card forms with the grades they want to see on their next report cards—twice a day for the next seven days.

7. Have the students put a copy of their report card in an envelope and address it to themselves. Collect these envelopes for safe keeping. At the end of the reporting period return the report cards to the students and discuss the process.

# 75

## Secret Number 4, FITS
## Follow Instructions To Success

> **W**hen all else fails, follow directions.
>
> —Anonymous

### Purpose

This activity is intended to help students be more effective by showing them the value in following directions.

### Materials Needed

Beforehand, collect a group of common, inexpensive household items for use by the groups. The objects chosen should have a specific, clearly understood use, so that students will know how to explain the operating instructions. Possible objects include the following:

- hand eggbeater
- compass

- dice
- stopwatch
- hand-held pencil sharpener
- hand can opener
- hinge
- curling iron
- spray bottle
- roll of tape
- thermometer
- tweezers
- band-aid
- video cassette

Place the objects in paper bags.

## Procedure

1. Introduce the activity by leading the following discussion: "Do you own a stereo, a walkman, a hair dryer, or any similar piece of mechanical equipment?

   "If so, you may have seen the booklet that comes with the equipment. It usually is called the operating instructions. Operating instructions are the information you need to know in order to have the machine work properly for you. If you don't know the operating instructions—or if you refuse to follow them even though you know what they are—you may risk injury. At best, the machine probably will not perform as intended.

   "The interesting thing about operating instructions is that they aren't just for machines. Everything—and everyone—has operating instructions. If you can discover what they are and follow the instructions, your life will be much happier, more hassle-free, and more successful than if you ignore them."

2. Write on the chalkboard, "Secret Number 4, FITS." Let students know that they will discover what this means later.

3. Have students form groups of five.

4. Give each group a paper bag containing an object, and warn each group, "Do not let any other group know what object is in your bag. Each group has a different object."

5. Continue with the instructions: "*Without* taking it out of the bag, identify the object and figure out what it is used for."

6. "Once you know what the object is, develop a list of operating instructions for the object. (Your list of operating instructions are the step-by-step directions you give to a person who is using the object for the first time.)"

7. "In writing your operating instructions, there are some things you may *not* say: you may not *name* the object; you may not tell the *purpose* of the object; and you may not use words that are obvious *giveaways*. The idea is to give step-by-step directions for using the object.

   "For example, if your object were a pencil sharpener, you could not say that it is used to sharpen pencils. Nor could you use the word *pencil* at all. You could, however, give these instructions:

   • 'Hold the object in your right hand with the hole pointed away from you.
   • 'Take the second object on which you are performing the action, and hold it in your left hand.
   • 'Insert the object in your left hand into the hole in the first object.
   • 'Twist the object in your right hand in a clockwise direction while holding the object in your left hand motionless,' and so on.

8. "After you have agreed on the operating instructions, write them on a piece of paper and put the paper in the bag with the object."

9. Now have the students pull their chairs into a circle.

10. One at a time, a representative from each group will read aloud the operating instructions for the group's object. The job of the rest of the class is to guess what the object is. If the operating instructions are clear, others should be able to guess the object. If not, students may ask specific questions about the operating instructions until they figure out what the object is.

    Note: *The class may ask questions only after all the operating instructions for the object have been read and no one has guessed correctly. All questions must be worded so that they can be answered either yes or no. Questions must be related to the step-by-step directions only, not to the purpose of the object.*

11. Remind students of Secret Number 4, FITS, and tell them that they will find out what it means during the next activity.

# 76

# *Operating Instructions for Success*

## Purpose

Prisons are filled with people who were unwilling or unable to follow society's operating instructions. There is a direct link between how much ease we experience in life and the extent to which we are taking responsibility for following operating instructions. The purpose of this activity is for students to realize the connection of operating instructions with the areas where they are being successful.

## Procedure

1. Ask each student to think of an activity he or she does well. It may be playing a game, sport or musical instrument, building models or fixing cars, styling hair, cooking a special dish, and so on.

2. Ask the students to identify what instructions they would give to someone else who wanted to be successful in their area of expertise.

3. Now have them consider some things that they would advise people *not* to do if they wanted to do well in this activity.

4. Have students get into their support groups and share the operating instructions in each of their areas.

5. Next, ask each student to identify an area in their lives where they are *not* experiencing success. You may suggest that they refer to the "Life Assessment Worksheet" for ideas.

6. Have them write down any operating instructions they have not been following that might help them be more effective in this area.

7. If they don't know what to do to be successful in this area of their lives, suggest that they first write down questions that they have about succeeding in their area.

8. Then return the students to the same group to discuss these questions on areas of difficulty and get suggestions and support from others as to what might work.

9. Complete this activity with the whole class, inviting students to share the insights that they gained.

10. Explain that "Secret Number 4, FITS" means "Follow Instructions To Success."

## Operating Instructions for the Classroom

1. Now have the students consider what Operating Instructions would support the classroom in functioning smoothly. You may do this in a number of ways such as:
   - full class brainstorming session
   - support groups generating recommendations which are then combined into one final list for the entire class
   - each student writing a list. In pairs, these lists are combined into one that both students agree on. These two students join another pair to combine their lists and so on, until one final class list is established.

2. Be sure that the students understand that they each need to agree to follow the Operating Instructions if they are to work. You may:
   - have each student sign an individual contract which lists the Class Operating Instructions and/or
   - post the Operating Instructions on the class bulletin board and have the students sign at the bottom of the list.

   Note: For suggested guidelines, see Activity 23 in Volume I of this book.

**FRANK & ERNEST® by Bob Thaves**

# 77

# No Such Thing As Failure

*Thomas Edison invented the electric light bulb, but as a small child, age 7, his teacher said he was too stupid to learn.*

*When Thomas Edison invented the light bulb, he tried over 2000 experiments before he got it to work. A young reporter asked him how it felt to fail so many times. He said, "I never failed once. I invented the light bulb. It just happened to be a 2000-step process."*

## Purpose

The purpose of this exercise is to teach students that it is okay to make mistakes. Mistakes are just a natural part of any learning process. We need to be willing to make mistakes so that we can learn from them and go on to create greater success in our lives. If we are afraid to make mistakes, we will be frozen in non-action.

## Procedure

1. Ask the students to make a list of five or more mistakes they have made in their lives. Have them describe briefly what happened—ask them to consider any operating instructions they overlooked, what data were missing, and so on.

2. Have students get into their support groups and share their mistakes and what they have learned from them. Give one to two minutes per student.

3. Ask each group to pick one mistake and what was learned, and share the experience with the whole class.

# No Such Thing as Failure II

> **Abraham Lincoln**
>
> *F*ailed in business at age 31.
>
> Was defeated in a legislative race at age 32.
>
> Failed in business again at age 34.
>
> Overcame the death of his sweetheart at age 35.
>
> Had a nervous breakdown at age 36.
>
> Lost an election at age 38.
>
> Lost a congressional race at age 43.
>
> Lost a congressional race at age 48.
>
> Lost a senatorial race at age 55.
>
> Failed in an effort to become vice president at age 56.
>
> Lost a senatorial race at age 58.
>
> Was elected president of the United States at age 60.

# Purpose

This activity can show students how attitudes can affect progress, and how we function in the world in response to feedback.

# Procedure

1. Explain to the class that the world provides us with feedback all the time. This feedback lets us know whether we are on course or off course—whether we are on the right track to accomplishing our goals or not. Feedback from the world is called *external feedback*. In contrast, *internal feedback* is something we get from ourselves; it also lets us know if we're on track or not.

   *"External on course"* feedback can be getting an *A* on a test, having others appreciate us for a job well done, or accomplishing a task successfully. *"Internal on course"* feedback can be feeling good about ourselves, waking up in the morning and wanting to jump out of bed, feeling peaceful or joyful when we're with others.

   *"External off course"* feedback can be getting a *D* or an *F* on a test, receiving complaints about a job we did, or unsuccessfully completing tasks. *"Internal off course"* feedback can be having a headache at the end of the day, feeling nauseous before working on a project, or being unhappy.

2. To illustrate to the class how feedback works, select a student to be the "feedback mechanism." Direct the student in the following way:

   What I want you to do is to walk across the room and stand so that you are directly opposite to me. . . . Good. You are my goal. My job is to get to you. You will also be my feedback mechanism. Your job is to provide a constant stream of feedback like a broken record. You will say 'on course' every time I move in a straight line directly toward you. You will say 'off course' if I do anything else. Clear? Okay. Ready? Begin. *(Pause.)*

   Do not move. Just stand there. The student will begin the steady stream of feedback, but will "peter-out" after a few seconds. Ask, "Why did you stop?"

   Invariably the student will answer, "Because you weren't moving." At which point say to the class:

   Ah ha! Lesson Number 1. The universe only responds to *action!* In the book, *In Search of Excellence,* Tom Peters talks about the top companies in America as having a 'Ready—Fire—Aim' action plan. They shoot first, and then take corrective action. Most people play this game: 'Ready—Aim—

118

Aim—' and they never do anything, so they can't get feedback. So Lesson Number 1 is: 'In order to get feedback, you must *do something!*'
Okay, *(volunteer)*, let's do this again.

With your first step, the student should begin a steady stream of *"on course, off course."* This time, move toward the student in a zigzag fashion, making sure you are *"off course"* more of the time than *"on course."* When you reach the student (your goal), turn to the class and ask, "Was I *on course* or *off course* more of the time?" ("Off course.") You respond, "Did I reach my goal?" They will answer yes. Say:

Remember that! I was off course most of the time, but I still reached my goal. The object is to complete a task successfully, not to avoid errors along the way. In doing anything the first, second, and even third time, people make mistakes. That's how they learn. There is no such thing as failure. There is only a delay in results. This is only an opportunity to learn how to do it better next time. Let me show you some ineffective ways to respond to feedback.

Here are some examples to demonstrate ineffective ways of responding to feedback.

## The Freakout

Move toward the student providing feedback. Veer *off* course and continue *off course* even though the student says, *"Off course."* Instead of correcting your movements, freak out, throwing your arms into the air and screaming:

"ARRRRGH! I can't take it anymore—it's too hard! Waaaaa!"

Ask the class, "Do any of you handle feedback in this manner?"

## Attack the Source of the Feedback

Move toward the student providing feedback. Veer *off course* and continue *off course*. Instead of correcting your movements, put your hands on your hips and yell at the student,

"Complain, complain, complain! Is that all you ever do? Don't you ever say anything nice?"

119

Ask the class, "Do any of you ever react to corrective suggestions in this way?"

## "I Don't Care What You Say, I'm Right!"

Move toward the student providing feedback. Veer *off course*. Instead of correcting your movement, plug both your ears and continue in the wrong direction. Ask the students, "Do any of you ignore the signs that say you are heading in the wrong direction? Do you ever continue to make mistakes rather than take corrective measures? Do you ever shut people out who might have valuable feedback for you? Your parents, teachers, coaches, or friends?"

## The Most Effective Way to Use Feedback

This time move toward the student providing feedback deliberately, slowly, one step at a time. Veer off course, and as soon as the student says, "*Off course,*" immediately stop. Tentatively put one foot out in several different *off course* directions, but without forward movement. Then place your foot directly *on course*, hear the feedback, and continue slowly, deliberately forward.

Continue the process of going *off course*, listening and testing, and moving back *on course* until you reach the student. Have students discuss what they have seen. Point out that the most efficient way to reach a goal is to listen to the feedback and to correct for any *off course* information.

# 78

## *Secret Number 5, CUP Commitment Unlocks Power*

> *U*ntil one is committed, there is hesitancy, the chance to draw back, always ineffectiveness. Concerning all acts of initiative (and creation), there is one elementary truth, the ignorance of which kills countless ideas and splendid plans; that the moment one definitely commits oneself, then Providence moves too. All sorts of things occur to help one that would never otherwise have occurred. A whole stream of events issues from the decision, raising in one's favor all manner of unforeseen incidents and meetings and material assistance, which no man could have dreamed would have come his way.
>
> —W. H. Murray, the Scottish Himalayan expedition

### Purpose

Commitment is the final secret, the last of the five-step process of achieving success. In many ways, it's the most important step of all.

People who are in love think about commitment. So do people who are entering a challenging career, such as medicine or law. And athletes must make a commitment to their sport if they intend to be any good.

Commitment is a type of promise that you make to yourself—and often to other people—to hang in there and keep working toward your goal even when the going gets tough. When you are committed, you want the result so much, it is so important to you, that you are willing to put up with discomforts and inconveniences you'd never stand for otherwise. Commitment is what creates families, wins games, invents new technology, makes art, and gives life its value.

Some people shy away from commitment. They are afraid of making promises. Maybe they don't trust themselves to keep their word. But the truth is commitment doesn't tie you down. Instead, it frees you to do your best. Ask Olympic athletes. Commitment is what drives them to exceed previous limits and to accomplish what no one has accomplished before.

Through this activity, students will learn about the power of keeping their word.

## Procedure

1. Write on the chalkboard, "Secret Number 5, CUP." Let them know that they will discover what this means by the end of the activity.

2. Distribute and ask students to fill out the Commitments Worksheet.

3. Have them share their responses in small groups.

4. Then, in the full class group, have each student state his or her commitment.

5. Discuss with students the other areas in their lives where they have commitments. Tell them that "Secret Number 5, CUP" means "Commitment Unlocks Power."

# COMMITMENTS WORKSHEET

Commitment means making a promise that you will be there for someone. It also means giving your word to do what you say you are going to do.

Think about your life right now. In what areas of your life are you committed? (You may not have made a verbal promise, but you are committed if you feel the commitment in your heart.)

What commitments do you have to your family?

_____

_____

_____

What commitments do you have to your friends?

_____

_____

_____

What commitments do you have as a student?

_____

_____

_____

What commitments do you have to develop your skills and talents in a particular field?

_____

_____

_____

What commitments do you have to yourself?

_____

_____

_____

What commitments do other people have to you? In other words, whom can you count on? For what?

_____

_____

_____

Has anyone ever made a promise to you and broken it? How did you feel? What price did you pay? What price did they pay?

_____

_____

_____

Have you ever broken a promise to someone else? How did you feel about that?

_____

_____

_____

Now is your chance to make a commitment. As a member of this class, you have an opportunity to make a real contribution. What is your commitment to your class, your school, and your community? Write your commitment statement here.

*I commit myself to* _____

_____

# 79

# Commitment Convention

## Purpose

This activity helps students realize the importance of commitments as social contracts that allow people to live and work together in support of everyone's life, liberty, and pursuit of happiness.

## Procedure

### Part One

1.  Introduce the activity by leading this discussion:

    - "Some of you may be familiar with the story of how the U.S. Constitution was written.
    - "After the Revolutionary War, the states were operating semi-independently. In some ways they worked together, but many problems arose because they thought of themselves as separate and independent governments.
    - "By the time they came together in 1789 to write the Constitution, they had decided it was time to give up some of their individual independence, 'in order to form a more perfect Union.' They also were ready to commit themselves to supporting each other and staying together, *no matter what*.
    - "Take a look at a copy of the Constitution. You'll notice that it has a preamble. The preamble is an inspirational statement, outlining the broad ongoing *purpose* of the government. The body of the Constitution, the articles and amendments, states the *operating*

*instructions* for the government. And the final page of the document includes the signatures of the authors, which represent their *commitment*. In this next activity, you are going to stage a convention of your own to draft a constitution for this class."

2. Continue with these directions:

   - "Get into a group of five people." (You may want to use the buddy groups.)
   - "Your group represents one of the states in the union. You can give your state any name you like." (It doesn't have to be named for one of the United States.)
   - "With your group, design a flag, and select a state animal, state color, and a state slogan. Later at the convention, your team will do a presentation to the others telling them about your state and showing them its various symbols.
   - "Decide what your team needs to do to be prepared for the presentation. Before class is over, write out a statement of commitment that each of you signs, pledging yourselves to do whatever is needed to make the presentation a success."

## Part Two

3. Now for the presentations:

   - "Get into a class circle for your state presentations.
   - "Elect a chairperson and a recorder to run the meeting.
   - "One at a time, the states will give their presentations, explaining the name of their state, its symbols, and anything else they want to say about its history, achievements, or greatness." *(Allow about five minutes for each group.)*
   - "After the presentations, the chairperson will assign your state to work on a draft for the preamble of your constitution.
   - "Bring your draft back to the convention when it is ready." *(Allow five to ten minutes.)*
   - "Each state will read its draft, and the group will decide on the wording for a final version.
   - "Next, your state will be asked to look at a particular area of the operating instructions for this class. You will write your operating instructions as one article of the constitution.
   - "When your article is complete, bring the draft back to the convention."

4. One at a time, the states will present their articles to the convention for revision, if necessary, and adoption.

5. When the final document is completed, it will be passed around the convention to be signed. Tell students, "Your signature is your commitment to support the constitution of the class."

   **Note:** *It may not be possible to finish the convention in one class period, depending on the length of your classes. If necessary, the convention can be extended for one or more days.*

   Complete this activity by reminding students that "Secret Number 5, CUP" means "Commitment Unlocks Power."

*There's a difference between interest and commitment. When you're interested in doing something, you do it only when it's convenient. When you're committed to something, you accept no excuses, only results.*

—Ken Blanchard

## 80

# *Awards Ceremony*

> *Silent gratitude isn't very much use to anyone.*
>
> —G. B. Stern

## Purpose

One secret successful people know is that no one is a success all alone. You always need the support and encouragement of other people, as well as direct actions they do for you, in order to make any project a success.

This activity is for students to acknowledge the people in the class for their leadership, good ideas, friendship, and help.

## Procedure

1. Divide the class into small groups.

2. Give each group the names of five other people in the class to acknowledge at the awards ceremony.

3. Ask the students when they get the names not to let anyone know

whose acknowledgments they are going to do. A surprise will make it more fun.

4. Instruct each group to take the names one at a time. "Consider all the specific actions the person has done during the course of the last unit that were helpful, useful, thoughtful, or in any other way a contribution to you personally or to the class.

5. "Also consider the things about the person that you like, admire, and appreciate; those things that make the person special."

6. Now that they have a list of qualities and contributions for which to acknowledge the person, direct them to think of a way of summarizing, in the form of a special award, what that person has done for the group. For example, there might be a person who gets the *thoughtfulness award* for always being kind to people, helping people who are having problems, and so on. Or there might be a *good humor award* for a person who lightens up heavy situations, and is always good for a laugh.

7. The group members are to think of the special award they want to give each person. Then think of a suitable form for the award. It could be a certificate, a trophy, an object, a picture, and so on. Whatever they select should be something that the group can make or find without too much difficulty. (You may want to give them some time to discuss what awards they need, and then assign the actual making of the awards as a homework assignment.)

8. When all the groups are finished, they are to bring their awards to the awards ceremony (class circle). You, as master of ceremonies, will call on each group to make their awards. If they want to, they can pretend they are Oscar presenters and call for "The envelope, please." That might add to the fun. Be sure that each group does a good job of explaining and displaying the award and letting the winner feel the full sincerity of their acknowledgment.

9. You may want to close with a discussion of questions such as:

   • "What award did you receive at the awards ceremony?"
   • "Do you know what people were acknowledging about you?"
   • "Do you ever acknowledge yourself for these good qualities? If you don't, take the time to do that now."

## Follow-Up Activity

Students can list people in their lives who deserve to be acknowledged for the things they have done for the students in the past month. The students could then be encouraged to make awards for these people or in some other creative way acknowledge these people for their contributions.

> *By appreciation, we make excellence in others our own property.*
>
> —Voltaire

BENT OFFERINGS by Don Addis. By permission of Don Addis and Creators Syndicate.

# CHAPTER SEVEN

## Social Responsibility

### Classroom as Community

*I can only close the gap in broken community by meeting hate with love. If I meet hate with hate, I become depersonalized, because creation is so designed that my personality can only be fulfilled in the context of community. When I love, I restore community.*

—Martin Luther King, Jr.

# INTRODUCTION

*People acting together as a group can accomplish things which no individual acting alone could ever hope to bring about.*

—Franklin D. Roosevelt

SCHOOLS DO NOT EXIST IN ISOLATION. They exist in communities and, for better or worse, they are affected by the social dynamics of the community. The challenges of crime, violence, substance abuse, poverty, and racial tension can be felt in many schools.

Although some people are resigned to the fact that schools reflect society, we authors are inspired by the possibility that schools can transform society. In every classroom, teachers have access to students who represent the next generation of world citizens. This is a spectacular opportunity to make a significant difference.

What if we all could work together with today's youth to discover how to establish a society in which everyone is valued, everyone contributes in a responsible manner, and everyone's needs and wants are met?

This chapter seeks to establish the framework of classroom as community. It is meant to encourage us all to continue to dream of a better world, and to recommit ourselves to making it real—starting here, starting now.

If you have not already done so, this would be a good time to apply the five "Secrets of Success" to creating and maintaining an effective, responsible classroom environment. Let's look at how to do that.

*Secret Number 1, GROE*
*Get Rid Of Expectations*

By now, any expectations that students had regarding this class have probably surfaced and been addressed. In some cases, unfulfilled expectations may have resulted in students getting upset. The "Collaborative Problem Solving" and "Conflict Management" sections of this chapter should prove useful in resolving issues based on unmet expectations.

*Secret Number 2, S = P × C*
*Satisfaction = Purpose × Clarity*

The purpose of your class ought to be clear to everyone, posted in the room, referred to frequently, and reflected in the activities that occur.

## Secret Number 3, WIN
### With INtention

By now, the students should be constantly setting goals, monitoring progress, and celebrating their successes. Maintaining a goals bulletin board or individualized goals folders for each student are ways of supporting this. Activity 89, "Peer Coaching—Goals Update," is a particularly effective way of empowering students' goal attainment.

## Secret Number 4, FITS
### Follow Instructions To Success

Class operating instructions should be identified (with full student involvement), posted, and used in a consistent manner to manage classroom functioning.

The "Team Effectiveness Check" (Activity 88) will give students an opportunity to reflect on how their behavior is contributing to class effectiveness.

## Secret Number 5, CUP
### Commitment Unlocks Power

All students should have made a commitment to supporting the class purpose and goals, and to following the operating instructions. The commitment could be in the form of a group declaration posted in the room or in the form of individual contracts.

Activity 90, "Peer Coaching—Keeping Commitments," in this chapter will help students support each other in living up to their responsibilities.

This chapter begins with a section on communication, which is appropriate, because *communication* and *community* both come from the same Latin word meaning to share or have in common.

In a most fundamental sense, education is communication. True communication is based on responsibility, a commitment to share a common framework, experience, or understanding. Responsible communication involves creating a relationship in which the partners form a bond—based on mutual respect—for a shared purpose.

This is very different from the all-too-familiar type of communication—which might be more accurately labeled *manipulation*—in which the purpose of the communication is to serve one's own ends; to look good, to be right, to say what you think is expected, or to get the other to say what you want to hear.

Effective communication is essential not only between teacher and student but also among the students as well. It is perhaps the single most important skill for functioning successfully in the world.

The purpose of this chapter is to support you in creating the conditions in your classroom for true community; conditions of responsible communication, trust, peer coaching, creative problem solving, and conflict resolution.

### All I Ever Really Needed to Know I Learned in Kindergarten

*Most of what I really need to know about how to live, and what to do, and how to be, I learned in kindergarten. Wisdom was not at the top of the graduate mountain, but there in the sandbox at nursery school.*

*These are the things I learned: Share everything. Play fair. Don't hit people. Put things back where you found them. Clean up your own mess. Don't take things that aren't yours. Say you're sorry when you hurt somebody. Wash your hands before you eat. Flush. Warm cookies and cold milk are good for you. Live a balanced life. Learn some and think some and draw and paint and sing and dance and play and work every day some.*

*Take a nap every afternoon. When you go out in the world, watch for traffic, hold hands, and stick together. Be aware of wonder. Remember the little seed in the plastic cup. The roots go down and the plant goes up and nobody really knows how or why, but we are all like that.*

*Goldfish and hamsters and white mice and even the little seed in the plastic cup—They all die. So do we.*

*And then remember the book about Dick and Jane and the first word you learned, the biggest word of all: LOOK. Everything you need to know is in there somewhere. The Golden Rule and love and basic sanitation. Ecology and plants and sane living.*

*Think of what a better world it would be if we all—the whole world—had cookies and milk about 3 o'clock every afternoon and then lay down on our blankets for a nap. Or if we had a basic policy in our nations to always put things back where we found them and cleaned up after our own messes. And it is still true, no matter how old you are, when you go out into the world, it is better to hold hands and stick together.*

—Robert Fulghum

# 81

# *Circle Talks*

> ***S****eek first to understand, then to be understood.*
>
> —Stephen Covey

One cornerstone of a comprehensive approach to building and maintaining high self-esteem is the use of "circle talks." Circle talks are conducted in small support groups, usually four to six students in size. In a circle talk, students share their thoughts and feelings about a particular topic, usually chosen by the teacher.

## Purpose

Circle talks give students an opportunity to express their thoughts and feelings in a safe and nurturing setting.

The positive benefits of circle talks are:

---

This activity was originally printed in *Self-Esteem in the Classroom* by Jack Canfield et al., and published by Self-Esteem Seminars in Culver City, CA. It is used here with permission.

- Students learn how to share their feelings rather than repress them. This is important in preventing teen suicide and drug abuse.
- Students learn valuable listening skills that can be applied to all relationships.
- Shyer, more reticent students are provided a safe structure for communication, which assures them an opportunity to express themselves and be heard. (One of the greatest problems in U.S. education is that many students suffer from a deficit of positive attention.)
- From others, students learn about additional coping behaviors and life attitudes that they can apply to their own life situations.
- Students discover that they are not alone in their feelings and that there are, indeed, universal situations and challenges everyone faces. As a result, students build deeper friendships with their peers, and unnecessary feelings of loneliness and isolation are overcome, thus building self-esteem and inner emotional strength to resist depression, drug abuse, teen suicide, and unwanted teen pregnancy.

Many students live in an isolated world, suffering from what Harry Stack Sullivan, a Harvard psychologist, called a "delusion of uniqueness"—a false belief that they alone suffer certain emotional stresses and life crises (such as divorced parents, alcoholic homes, sibling rivalry, fear of failure, loneliness, stress at school, disappointments in athletic and academic achievement, teasing, lack of money, fear of rejection, fear of participating in certain activities, hopes and dreams that are not supported, and so on). When students discover that others also have these same longings, fears, conflicts, and doubts, they no longer feel alone. Instead, they feel bolstered by the realization that these things are shared with others. This, in turn, helps them to accept and feel comfortable with their own emotions. Such students no longer think of themselves and their feelings as strange, weird, or unacceptable. Self-acceptance, self-expression, and self-confidence are nurtured and expanded, and students feel free to turn their attention to their schoolwork.

Another benefit is that teachers who regularly conduct circle talks in their classrooms begin to know their students at a much deeper level. They begin to better understand the causes of their students' behavior, their hidden motivations, their fears, and their desires. Teachers find they have more information to use in individualizing their instruction, and in helping students overcome what may appear to be "learning blocks."

## Procedure

1.  Gather students into groups of four to six each. These may be their support groups or newly formed groups. Each group is given a "focus object," which is used to indicate whose turn it is to speak. Objects that have been used successfully are heart-shaped bean bags (these hearts, which we prefer, can be ordered for $10 each from Self-Esteem Seminars, 6035 Bristol Parkway, Suite G, Culver City, CA 90230), teddy bears, stuffed animals, tennis balls, Native American peace pipes, baseballs or rocks. The object serves the purpose of visually denoting whose turn it is to talk and it gives the speaker something to "hold on to."

While one student is holding the object, everyone else remains silent. The object acts as a visual reminder that no one may interrupt the speaker. Students learn to wait their turn by waiting for the object to reach them. Students also report that holding the focus object makes it easier to speak. It gives their hands something to do and is comforting.

2.  Introduce the guidelines to the students.

    *   "Only the person holding the object may talk. Everyone else is to remain silent and give the speaker their complete attention and support.
    *   "Pass the object gently to the left. The object is never to be thrown from one person to another.
    *   "You have the right to 'pass.' There is no requirement or pressure to share. Just say, 'I pass,' and pass the object to the person on your left.

- "Talk only about what you think and feel. Do not talk about what other people have said. Focus on your feelings about a topic.
- "No put-downs. Listen to the speaker without judgment or criticism.
- "Keep confidentiality—do not share what is said here outside of your group.
- "Talk as long as you need to, but be aware that other people want a turn also.
- "Do not leave the group during the circle talk."

In Grades 5 to 12, we suggest that you post the circle talk guidelines in your classroom so that students can refer to them as needed.

3. Ask the students if they have any questions about the guidelines. Tell them they may find it difficult to listen without interrupting at first, and that there is great value in learning how to give others their total attention. If you have the time, you may also wish to lead a brief discussion using the following questions as discussion starters:

- "All of you have experienced somebody not paying attention when you were talking. (Perhaps the other person was distracted by TV or by someone else.) How do you feel when someone looks away when you are talking to him or her? Does it make you feel less important? Does it make you feel angry?
- "And all of you have had the experience of talking about something really important to you and having someone interrupt you to start talking about what he or she wanted to say. Has anyone ever taken the focus away from you in a group discussion, for example? Did you like that? How did you feel? What did you want instead?"

The fact is that we all yearn to be listened to, understood, and accepted by others. We all need to be the center of attention on a regular basis. In order to receive attention, we must also learn to give it to others. True listening is one of the greatest gifts we can give another person.

4. After you have introduced the guidelines, make sure that everyone understands them and is willing to play by the rules. If certain students do not agree to the guidelines, ask them to sit outside of their circle or group, and give them quiet desk work to do. Emphasize to the whole class that their decision not to participate is acceptable.

## How Long Should a Circle Talk Last?

The length of a circle talk depends on several things—the age and maturity level of the students, the interest level and intensity of students on the topic under discussion, and the time available for the activity. In general, a circle talk lasts 8–14 minutes. Students continue to pass the focus object around the circle, with students taking repeated turns until the time has elapsed, thus assuring that all groups end at the same time. It is usually a good idea to tell the class when half the time has elapsed, giving the students an opportunity to speed things up if less than half the group has shared.

If your time frame is open-ended, you can continue the circle talk until everyone says, "I pass," indicating that there is no more to be said on the subject, or you can limit the passing of the focus object to one round.

If there is time after a circle talk, it can be valuable to discuss what students learned from the circle talk.

## When to Conduct Circle Talks

There are two times to use circle talks in your classroom. The first is before or after any kind of emotional upset. These occasions can include the following:

- death of a classmate
- loss of a major athletic event
- fight or bout of teasing
- when a major privilege has been taken away
- when a lot of students have failed a test
- interracial incident
- loss of a pet or class mascot
- cancellation of a field trip due to bad weather
- viewing an emotionally stimulating film
- reading a particularly emotional passage
- announcement of the election of class officers
- dissection of an animal in biology class
- heated political debate in a social sciences class
- SAT tests or final exams

Perhaps even more important is the use of circle talks in a developmental way. We suggest conducting circle talks one to three times a week, depending on the class and the time available. We believe once a week is the absolute minimum for effectively building high self-esteem and responsible communication.

## Topics for Circle Talks

When you are first beginning to use circle talks, you may choose to begin with simple, positively focused topics. For example, students could discuss:

1. a success I recently had (during the summer, last year, and so on)
2. what I would do if I won the state lottery (inherited $1 million, and so on)
3. where I would like to live if I could live anywhere in the world
4. something I would like to achieve in the next three years
5. my favorite movie, TV show, song (favorite anything)
6. something I like about myself
7. how I feel about doing a circle talk
8. something I wish I could do better
9. my favorite thing to do
10. a fun thing that happened this week
11. something I am good at doing
12. something I have always wanted to do
13. something I think about a lot
14. if I had three wishes, what they would be
15. something I wished for that came true.

Here are some more topics:

16. something about my physical appearance that makes me feel okay
17. something about my physical appearance that makes me feel not okay
18. something I don't like about myself
19. something I sometimes wonder about
20. an especially good dream I had
21. an especially bad dream I had
22. something I sometimes worry about
23. a way I get over being afraid
24. a time I was afraid
25. a time I was scared and it was fun
26. a time I was scared and it wasn't fun

27. a good result of something I do
28. a bad result of something I do
29. something that makes me angry with myself
30. what I do when I'm very angry
31. what I do when I'm very afraid
32. something I feel sad about
33. what I do when I am sad
34. a time I acted like a leader
35. a time I enjoyed being a follower
36. a time I had to struggle with someone for power, and I won
37. a time I had to struggle with someone for power, and I lost
38. the most fun I've ever had
39. the worst trouble I ever got into
40. a time when I couldn't get what I needed
41. a time when I knew the truth and lied anyway . . . and what happened
42. a time when I told the truth even though it was difficult
43. a way I have of getting attention from others
44. a decision I made that was very hard to make
45. a decision I had to make where either way it seemed like I would lose
46. a decision I had to make between things I wanted very much
47. a time I said no to peer pressure
48. a time I had to resist others to do what I wanted
49. a time I helped to change a rule or policy
50. something I did that helped someone else feel good
51. something that someone did for me that helped me feel good
52. the things I do to keep a friend
53. a time I found a way to meet someone I wanted to know
54. a time I got someone else to change his or her mind about something
55. a time I did something that someone else did not like
56. a time I wanted attention and did not get it
57. a time I gave someone attention because he or she needed it
58. a time I didn't know how to get attention
59. a time I was new and didn't know how to break into the circle
60. a time someone did something that helped me feel included
61. a time when I did something that helped someone feel included
62. a time I did something that excluded someone
63. a time when I felt excluded or left out
64. a time I made a promise and did not keep it

65. a time someone made a promise to me and did not keep it
66. a time I kept my word
67. how someone hurt my feelings
68. a time I did not know how to ask for a favor
69. a time I told someone something but did not mean it
70. a time when someone was disappointed in me
71. a time I was disappointed in someone else
72. something I have to do that I don't like to do
73. a time I went along with the crowd, even though I didn't like it
74. something I can't stand in people
75. something I do that bugs other people
76. something that I appreciate about my parents
77. a time I resisted authority
78. something it's hard to "go against the crowd" about
79. something I did that someone else criticized
80. how I get people to do what I want them to do
81. a secret fear I have
82. a secret wish I have
83. how I feel about war (or the homeless, the environment, teacher–student relationships, parent–student relationships, boy–girl relationships, cliques, gangs, drugs, dress codes, homework, this school, and so on).

*Note: When dealing with issue-related circle talks, it is important to remember that the purpose is not to obtain agreements of any sort. This is not a rap session or a discussion. Each person merely states his or her feelings about the issue. The emphasis is on listening to one another's feelings and, through that experience, discovering more about one's own feelings. Remember, this is a feeling exercise, so thoughts and opinions, although acknowledged, are not the primary focus. Circle talks are not meant to clarify thoughts and opinions (although they often do), but rather to introduce and provide practice in how to talk about and listen to each other's feelings.*

# DENNIS THE MENACE

"HOW DO YOU EXPECT ME TO HEAR YOU WHEN I WASN'T EVEN *LISTENING* ?"

## 82

# *Spending Money*

## *Purpose*

The purpose of this activity is for students to practice effective listening skills in a group problem-solving situation.

## *Procedure*

1. Divide the class into teams of six or seven.

2. Have each group select a moderator who will be in charge of making sure that everyone follows the operating instructions. This student will not otherwise get involved in the discussion.

3. Hand out copies of Effective Listening Skills and discuss these with the students.

4. Hand out copies of the Spending Money Worksheet.

5. Describe the simulated situation to the students. The class has just received a donation of $100 from a wealthy member of the community. Their task is to decide how to spend the $100. The worksheet specifies the available options. The team has 20 minutes to reach a consensus on how to spend the money. If they are unable to decide within that time frame, the money will be given to another class instead.

6. The one other operating instruction is that before any student can state his or her point of view, he or she must restate and validate the point made by the person who spoke just before him or her. The moderator's job is to make sure this happens.

7. Give a two-minute warning before the end of the time period, and then call time at the end of the 20 minutes.

8. Have someone from each group report on what option the group decided on and the process used to arrive at it.

9. Engage the entire class in a discussion of effective listening skills and how they affect group process.

   • In what ways was it helpful?
   • Were there times when it got in the way?
   • How can these skills be applied in other areas of their lives?

**E**

### Encourage
- Tell me more.
- What you are saying is important to me, please continue.
- What else do you want to say?
- When did it happen?
- Where did it happen?
- How did you feel about it?

**A**

### Acknowledge
- I appreciate what you are saying.
- I understand how you must have felt.
- I think your point of view is important.
- I accept your perception of the situation as valid.
- Thank you for letting me know.
- Thank you for trusting me enough to confide in me.

**R**

### Restate
- Are you saying that . . . ?
- Am I understanding you correctly that . . . ?
- Do you mean to say that . . . ?
- I get the sense that you are frustrated; is this accurate?
- You seem quite upset; is this true?
- So what you are saying is . . . and how you feel about it is. . . .

**S**

### Summarize
- So, what I've heard so far is . . .
- Let me see if I got this accurately; so far you've said that . . .
- So your point, as I understand it, is . . .
- The key issues seem to be . . . Is this true?
- What I've heard thus far suggests to me that your major concerns are . . .
- To bring closure to our conversation, let me summarize what we've discussed.

Your class has received a $100 donation from a wealthy member of the community. As a group, you must decide on how to spend the money from among the options listed below.

You have 20 minutes to come to a decision, otherwise the money will be given to another class. Your group must all agree on the choice.

*Options:*

1. Divide the money equally among all the class members.

2. Use the money to pay for a field trip related to a class project.

3. Give the money to the physical education department for more sports equipment.

4. Use the money to buy toys for a program like Toys for Tots for children less fortunate than yourselves.

5. Donate the money to an organization that provides meals for AIDS patients who are not well enough to care for themselves.

6. Use the money to buy blankets and distribute them to people who are homeless.

7. Use the money to set up a recycling program to help save the environment.

8. Spend the money on a fun party for your class.

*Whatever kind of word thou speakest, the like shalt thou hear.*

—Greek proverb

**PEANUTS**/Charles Schulz

# 83

# Have a Heart

> **W**isdom is the reward you get for a lifetime of listening when you'd have preferred to talk.
>
> —Doug Larson

## Purpose

This activity is essentially the same as "Spending Money" and may be used as an alternate. The purpose, again, is to promote the use of effective communication skills—both listening and speaking—by using them in another simulation exercise.

## Procedure

1. Divide the class into teams of six or seven.

2. Have each group select a moderator who will be in charge of making sure that everyone follows the operating instructions. The moderator does not get involved in the discussion.

3. Review Effective Listening Skills (see preceding activity).

4. Hand out copies of the Have a Heart Worksheet.

5. Explain the simulated situation, and let the students know that they have 20 minutes to come up with a group decision.

6. The operating instruction about effective listening is that before anyone can state their own point of view, he or she must restate or validate what was just said by the previous speaker. In addition, every statement must be made responsibly; that is, "I" messages must be used. So, every statement must be preceded by phrases such as:

   • "I think . . ."
   • "I feel . . ."
   • "From my point of view . . ."
   • "The way I see it . . ."
   • "What I think is . . ."

7. Give a two-minute warning and then call time at the end of 20 minutes.

8. Have someone from each group report on the group's decision and the process used to arrive at it.

9. Bring the class together for a closing discussion of the issues raised and the importance of effective listening and speaking.

# Andy Capp

## By Reggie Smythe

153

Imagine that you are a group of surgeons at a big hospital. As a committee, you must make a very important decision. There is one heart donor at this time, and eight patients need a heart transplant. So far as we know, the prognosis for a successful transplant is the same for all the patients. Your committee must choose who will receive the transplant. You have 20 minutes to arrive at a group decision.

## Patients

1. A 17-year-old Chicana waitress; a high school dropout and the sole provider for her family

2. A 15-year-old pregnant woman; unmarried, white, and has no other children

3. An Hispanic high school senior, class president, who recently won a scholarship to medical school

4. A 24-year-old single mother with three young children; a Vietnamese widow with no other family in this country

5. A 52-year-old African American religious leader who runs a homeless shelter and soup kitchen that feeds thousands of people daily

6. A 40-year-old scientist close to discovering a cure for AIDS; a white male who is HIV positive himself

7. An 11-year-old Middle Eastern girl who has become a symbol for world peace

8. A transfer patient from a small rural medical facility—no other data available

Adapted with permission from *Training High School Conflict Managers*, copyright © 1986, The Community Board Program.

# 84

## Trust Walk

### Purpose

Trust is an essential quality for being in a relationship or part of a community. This is the first in a series of three exercises designed to increase students' ability to trust and be trusted. In all three activities, they will be delivering services that require others to trust them with their well-being. The responsibility is serious. Students must be willing to trust and be trusted. By trusting others, we empower each other and allow ourselves to become even more worthy of trust.

### Materials Needed

one blindfold (6- × 18-inch strip of cloth) for every two students

### Procedure

1. For this activity you will need to find a suitable area of the school. You will need a space large enough for the class to move around

freely in pairs without running into each other or other students. You also need some privacy from outsiders who might disrupt the activity. The space should have some variation in terrain—some slopes or stairs, different surfaces to walk on, and so on. However, it should not have any dangerous areas where students could be injured. Ideally the area would be open enough for you to observe the pairs as they walk. If there is no one area large enough, delegate students to be stationed in each area so that they can monitor the activity. Ideal places are the playground, a gymnasium, or a quiet wing of the school building.

2. Ask students to each find a partner.

3. Give them the following instructions: "You will take turns guiding each other on a trust walk. One of you will be blindfolded so that you cannot see where you are going. You will hold onto the arm of your guide and depend on that person's directions. When you are the guide, your job will be to give clear directions to the blindfolded person. Be patient and understanding. Consider what the person needs to know and how to make him or her feel comfortable and secure."

4. Before starting on the walk, discuss the risk factor and ask the students to communicate to their partner any concerns they have.

5. Have the group identify operating instructions that will allow the activity to be done safely.

6. Request that they make a serious commitment to each other to support their safety and well-being.

7. Once you reach the designated area, give each pair of students one blindfold. Tell them that they will take turns being the guide. Ask them to decide who is partner A and who is partner B. Partner A puts on the blindfold and takes the arm of partner B. Partner B leads partner A on the walk, giving instructions about where to step, obstacles in the way, and so on. After five to seven minutes, call time and have the students remove their blindfolds. Give the partners a few minutes to talk about their experience of leading and being led. Then have the partners change roles and continue the exercise.

8. After the second round of five to seven minutes, tell them to stop and remove their blindfolds. Once again, give them a few minutes to talk about their experiences. Have them acknowledge their partners for guiding them and also for trusting them. Ask them to discuss the following question: If you were going to do this activity again, what changes would you make? Suggest that they discuss answers to this question with their partners.

9.  Bring the class together in a circle for closure. Have them take turns sharing what it felt like to be blindfolded and also what it felt like to be the guide. Possible discussion questions:

    - "Did you feel fully comfortable and supported by your guide?"
    - "If not, what could your guide have done differently to make you feel more trusting?"
    - "What could you have done differently to make yourself feel more trusting of them?"
    - "How did it feel to have someone else depend on you? Did you feel worthy of the trust?"

## Variation

Divide the class into three groups of 10 people each. Everyone in the group is blindfolded except the leader. Place your right hand on the right shoulder of the person in front of you. Follow the leader, getting cues from the movements of the person in front of you. This should be done non-verbally.

# 85

# *Trust Pass*

## Purpose

This next activity in the trust-building exercises involves trusting a group of people, rather than just one other person. Sometimes in a group activity, people think their part doesn't count, that others will do it for them. In this activity, the group is no stronger than its weakest member. Students must trust themselves and be willing to be responsible for the well-being of others.

> **Note:** *Be sure students are dressed appropriately for this activity. Pants and shirts, or gym clothes, work best. Again, it is necessary to be in a place that has enough room and some privacy.*

## Procedure

1. The point of this activity is to pick up one person and pass the person overhead from one end of the group to the other, letting him or her down gently on the other end.

2. Choose one person to go first. The rest of the class should gather together to support this person being passed over their heads.

3. The student to be passed removes his or her shoes before starting. Then do a readiness check with the group. The person to be passed calls out, "Ready?" The group should reply, "Ready," in unison. If they aren't together, or if some people don't answer, the group isn't yet ready to be trusted with this student's well-being. Check in again, and wait until a positive response is received before starting.

4. The first two people in line, bend their knees and pick the person up, one of them holding under the arms and the other under the knees. They then stand up, holding the student securely before passing him or her on to the rest of the line.

5. When you are standing in line, hold your hands above your head, palms open, and gently support the person as he or she is passed slowly from one end of the group to the other. The person's weight should be distributed among three or more supporters. All students should be paying full attention and should feel totally responsible for each other's well-being. Students should call for additional support if they find themselves trying to hold the person alone.

6. When the first student gets to the other side, he or she puts his or her shoes back on and joins the group at the end.

7. People in front of the line are next up to be passed.

8. Continue until everyone has had the opportunity to be passed.

9. After the activity, have the students sit down and talk about the experience.

   • Invite them to acknowledge themselves for a job well done.
   • Ask them, if they were going to do this again, what changes, if any, would they make?
   • Have them share what it felt like to be passed over the heads of the group.
   • Did they have any fears before it happened?
   • How do they feel now?
   • What was it like to pass the person overhead?
   • Was it different from what they expected? In what ways?

# 86

# Trust Fall

> *T*rust is the result of a successfully survived risk.
>
> —Jack R. Gibb

## Purpose

This activity, building on the previous two, increases considerably the risk factor and hence the level of trust required.

> **Note:** *For this activity, you need to find two stable platforms about four feet off the ground from which students can fall backward. Safety is of the utmost importance. Since someone could get hurt if this is not done correctly, it is very important that you continually monitor both groups. If you feel uncomfortable, only do this with one group so you can more easily monitor the whole process or use student monitors who are familiar with the process and responsible for safety. We have done this exercise for 20 years and have never had anyone get hurt. It is extremely effective, in building trust and well worth the effort. If you have the slightest concern about whether the students are ready for this, don't attempt it!*

## Procedure

1.  Introduce this activity by saying, "By now, you should be feeling a fair amount of trust toward your classmates. Do you trust them enough to let them catch you as you fall? Do you trust them with your LIFE? Guess what you're going to be doing today!"

2.  Inform them that the object of today's activity is to let yourself fall backward and be caught by the group. Go over the entire sequence and practice all the steps leading up to the fall, to be sure that everyone understands.

    - "Form groups of 12 to 15.
    - "Decide who is going to go first.
    - "The rest of you, line up in a tight double line facing each other.
    - "Put your arms straight out at shoulder height, your arms alternating with the person's opposite you. This is so your two arms will not have to bear the faller's whole weight.
    - "Close your hands so that your fingers and thumbs won't get jammed.
    - "Wait for the ready signal.
    - "The first two people in line are responsible for making sure that the line is straight and in position to make the catch. If they don't feel comfortable about the position, they will answer, 'Not ready,' when the faller asks.
    - "When it is your turn to fall, climb up on the platform and state which of the following is true for you: 'I am freely choosing to do this activity' or 'I am freely choosing not to do this activity now.' If you choose not to do it, the group will acknowledge you for your choice.
    - "If you choose to do it, then get in position with your back to the group, and ask, 'Are you ready?'
    - "The group members respond, 'Ready!' if they are, 'Not ready!' if they are not. (If they are not ready, wait until they are.)
    - "Then, just to make double sure, say, 'Can I trust you with my life?'
    - "You should hear a resounding *yes!* If you don't, check in and find out what's happening.
    - "Before you actually fall, let them know you are coming. Say, 'Falling!' The group's response should be 'Fall on!' If this doesn't sound together enough, check in again before you fall.
    - "When you actually make your fall, keep your legs straight and

**161**

keep your body level. Lock your hands and hold your arms in front of you to avoid hitting someone when you fall.

- "When you are in the line and a person is falling toward you, keep your arms outstretched, hands clenched, and bend your knees slightly to absorb the weight. Once the person is caught, pass him or her gently along the line to the end, as you did with the trust pass, and let him or her down to rejoin the line.
- "If you feel like applauding, be sure to wait until the person's feet are firmly on the ground!
- "The people standing at the front of the line go up next. Continue rotating until everyone has had a turn."

3.  Bring the class together. Debrief what happened and how they felt. Have them acknowledge themselves for their successes.

- "If you were going to do the activity again, would you make any changes? If so, what?"
- "What did it feel like to fall and be caught by the group?"
- "Were you afraid beforehand that you would get hurt?"
- "Were you surprised at the feeling of being caught?"
- "How is your level of trust for the students in your class at this point?"
- "Do you have more feeling of team spirit than you had at the beginning of this unit on trust?"
- "If so, what specific experiences contributed most to the change?"
- "Think about other areas in your life where you have to trust other people for your well-being. How do you feel about those relationships?"
- "Do some changes need to be made to increase the level of trust?"
- "If so, what can you do to make those changes happen?"
- "Set a goal related to increasing your ability to trust and be trusted."

# 87

# *Every One Counts*

> *It really boils down to this: that all life is interrelated. We are all caught in an inescapable network of mutuality, tied into a single garment of destiny. Whatever affects one directly, affects all indirectly.*
>
> —Martin Luther King, Jr.

## Purpose

In this activity, students will appreciate the importance of working together as a team to accomplish a common goal. They will become aware of the relationship between personal success and group or team success, and will realize that by shifting from personal self-interest to concern for the needs of others, their own needs get taken care of in the process.

**Note:** *In advance, prepare sets of broken square puzzles as diagrammed.*

## Procedure

1.  Divide the class into groups of five students. (If there are extra students, establish a sixth student as necessary. Have this student

function as an "observer." The observer's job is to watch the process, notice how the team approaches putting together the puzzle, and be prepared to report during the debriefing.)

2. Tell them, "The purpose of this activity is for you to experience the interrelationship between personal success and group success. The goal of this activity is for each of you to put together a square that is equal in size to the square of everyone else on your team.

"The operating instructions are as follows:

- Players may not talk, point, or in any way communicate with the other people in the group.
- Players may give pieces to other participants, but may not just take pieces from another person.
- Players may not throw their pieces into the center for others to take; they must give the pieces directly to an individual.
- Players may give away pieces to their puzzle, even after they have already formed a square.

"In order for the game to work, each player must make a commitment to the purpose, goal, and operating instructions. Is there anyone not willing to follow the operating instructions?" (*Answer questions or concerns. If there are still some unwilling to participate, assign these students as observers.*) "Those of you who are observers are to watch the process, notice how the team approaches putting the puzzles together, and be prepared to report back to us."

3. Allow enough time for each group to complete the activity. Ask groups who are finished to wait quietly until the others are done. You might let the students who are finished talk among themselves about their experience of the activity. You might also ask them to give clues to the groups who are still working on the puzzle, without revealing too much and spoiling the fun of discovery.

4. Bring the class together to debrief:

- "What worked?"
- "What got in the way of success?"
- "Based on this experience, what would you say is important for individual success and group success?"

(Responses to the last question can be written on the board, under the heading "Guidelines for Individual and Group Success.")

5. You may want to make the following concluding remark: "This exercise serves as a model for how we can create a classroom, school,

and society where everybody wins. Recognizing that there is no scarcity, there are no missing pieces, we realize that the universe already has everything that any of us could need or want. We each have a contribution to make to the whole. We can each look at what other people need and give what we have to give. We can be open to what other people have contributed to us. Then, like magic, it all comes together. What is needed is a commitment to our own personal success and also a commitment to contribute to the success of everyone else in the class."

## Supplementary Activity

A nice way to end this activity is to read *Horton Hears a Who* to the class. This delightful book stresses this same theme—that everyone's contribution is important, that we are all indispensable pieces to the overall puzzle. (Dr. Seuss, *Horton Hears a Who*: New York: Random House, 1954.) The book takes about five minutes to read.

An easy way to have everyone see the pictures as you go along is to xerox each page of the book onto an overhead transparency and show that transparency as you read that page in the book. It will help hold the students' attention.

To make the puzzle pieces for this activity, use poster board or heavy coated paper. For each group of five or six students, cut five 6-inch squares. Using the following patterns, cut each of the squares into pieces. (Note: all the A's are the same size.)

Now, in order to mix the pieces up, put them in envelopes as follows:

*Envelope A:* pieces I, H, E    *Envelope B:* pieces A, A, A, C
*Envelope C:* pieces A, J     *Envelope D:* pieces D, F
*Envelope E:* pieces G, B, F, C

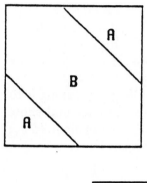
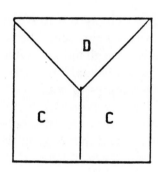
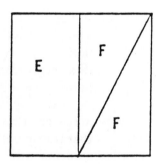

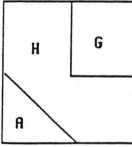
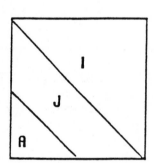

# Team Effectiveness Check

> *The main ingredient of stardom is the rest of the team.*
>
> —John Wooden, UCLA basketball coach

## Purpose

This activity encourages students to work as a team in being responsible for maintaining an effective classroom environment.

## Procedure

1. Fill in the class purpose and operating instructions (Activities 61 and 76) that the class agreed to on the Team Effectiveness Worksheet.

2. Duplicate the worksheet and distribute copies to the students.

3. Ask them to rate how well they and the class have been doing in keeping their agreements.

4. Instruct them to write down what they and the class can do to improve class effectiveness.

5.   Start with those areas where the students have been most successful by asking for the items that received the highest scores. Acknowledge these.

6.   Then focus on the areas that received the lowest scores. Discuss ways in which class effectiveness could be improved in these areas.

7.   Be open to revising the operating instructions if necessary.

8.   Solicit renewed commitment.

9.   Also have each student state individually what he or she intends to do to continue to improve class effectiveness.

# TEAM EFFECTIVENESS WORKSHEET

## Rate the class performance on a scale from 1 to 5.

| 1 | 2 | 3 | 4 | 5 |
|---|---|---|---|---|
| Poor | Adequate | Good | Very Good | Excellent |

**1.** To what extent do you feel the class is fulfilling its purpose?

*Class Purpose*

_____

_____

_____

_____

**2.** To what extent do you think the class is following the operating instructions?

| Class Operating Instructions | Team | Personal |
|---|---|---|
| _____ | _____ | _____ |
| _____ | _____ | _____ |
| _____ | _____ | _____ |
| _____ | _____ | _____ |

**3.** What recommendations do you have for improving class effectiveness?

_____

_____

**4.** What can you do personally to contribute to the class being a more effective team?

_____

_____

# 89

# Peer Coaching—Goals Update

## Purpose

This activity encourages students to support each other in successfully achieving their goals.

## Procedure

1. Distribute copies of the Peer Coaching—Goals Update Worksheet.

2. Have each student find a partner and decide who will go first.

3. Tell them to refer to one of their goals—this could be from the "Team Effectiveness Check" or from the previous section on success and happiness.

4. The students take turns in coaching each other on their goals by using the questions listed on the worksheet.

5. When the students are finished, have them gather together to debrief. Discuss other ways in which students can support each other in achieving their goals.

1. What was the goal you set for yourself?
2. Did you achieve it?
3. *If yes:* congratulations!
   - What specifically did you do?
   - To what do you owe your success?
   - How do you feel about your accomplishment?
   - What worked for you in support of your success?
   - What did you learn from this?
   - Were there any points along the way that were difficult and/or where things didn't work?
   - What did you learn from this?
   - Would you say this goal was too easy, too difficult, challenging yet realistic, enough of a stretch to be a real accomplishment?
   - Given your experience, what is your goal for the next period of time?

   *If no:*
   - What happened?
   - How do you feel about what happened?
   - In what way was this what you expected?
   - What happened that was unexpected?
   - What didn't work?
   - What did you learn from this?
   - Were there points along the way when you were successful?
   - What worked?
   - What did you learn from this?
   - What are the consequences of your not having achieved your goal?
   - Commitment check—on a scale of 1 to 10 how committed would you say you were?
   - Is this goal still important to you?
   - What is your purpose in accomplishing this?
   - Given your experience this time, how will you modify your goal?
   - What will you do differently in achieving the goal?
   - What operating instructions do you need to be responsible for?
   - What other resources or support do you feel you need?
   - Commitment check—on a scale of 1 to 10, how committed would you say you are now to accomplishing this goal?

4. Summarize the session, emphasizing the positives.

171

## THE FAR SIDE    By GARY LARSON

"Late again! . . . This better be good!"

# 90

# Peer Coaching—
# Keeping Commitments

## Purpose

This activity is intended to provide students with a technique to support each other in being responsible for keeping their agreements.

## Procedure

This activity may be done as a structured activity with the entire class or on an ad hoc basis when individual students run into difficulty in keeping their agreements or in following class operating instructions. The value of using peer coaching for this is that it encourages students to monitor each other and shifts your role from that of sole disciplinarian to that of a resource for students.

Use the Peer Coaching—Keeping Commitments handouts the way in which the Goals Update worksheet was used. One sheet is related to operating instructions, and the other is for following up on assignments.

1. Have the students find a partner and decide who will go first.

2. Have the students take turns coaching each other in following operating instructions or completing assignments by asking the questions on the Peer Coaching handouts.

3. When the students are finished, have them come together as a full group to share insights that they gained, to discuss questions that

they have, and to request any support they need to be responsible in keeping their agreements.

Since the purpose of this type of coaching is to increase the students' awareness of their behavior, and since awareness is best developed in an environment free from blame, guilt, or fear of punishment, the student coach should maintain an attitude of support by reflecting back to the other student what is being said, without judgment or evaluation.

The reference to consequences is also meant to be neutral. What will follow *naturally?* (If I jump off a building, I will fall down. No one is doing this *to* me. It is a natural consequence of my action. If I do not study, I will probably do poorly in the class. The teacher is not doing it *to* me. It merely follows.)

When the natural consequences are not sufficient to support the student in keeping his or her agreements, then a support system needs to be devised.

*Coach:*  What would work to support you in keeping your word?
*Student:*  I don't know.

*Coach:*  If you knew you would have to stay after school to complete the assigned work, would this support you in doing it beforehand?

*Student:*  Yes.

## OPERATING INSTRUCTIONS

**1. Ask, "What happened?"**

"What are you doing?" "Are you late?" "Are you talking?" and so on.

**2. Ask, "What is the operating instruction?"**

Relate his or her behavior to the agreed-on operating instruction.

**3. Summarize response to steps 1 and 2.**

"So you are late and you know that we have an agreement to be on time?"

**4. Ask, "Did you keep your agreement?"**

"Who is responsible for your keeping or not keeping your agreements?" "Are you meeting your responsibilities in this matter?"

**5. Ask, "Are you now willing to keep your commitment?"**

"What are you going to do from now on to meet your responsibilities?"

**6. Indicate consequences** (natural or agreed-on) for repeating the irresponsible behavior.

**7. Acknowledge your partner** for willingness to learn and grow in the area of responsibility.

## ASSIGNMENTS

**1.** What were your assignments?

_____

_____

_____

**2.** Did you complete them all?

_____

_____

**3.** *If yes,*
    a. How did you feel about it?

_____

_____

    b. What supported you in keeping your commitment?

_____

_____

    c. What did you learn about yourself?

_____

_____

**4.** *If no,*

   a. Did you make a commitment to do your assignments?

   _____

   _____

   b. What happened that you didn't do them?

   _____

   _____

   c. What was more important to you than keeping your word?

   _____

   _____

   d. How do you feel about that?

   _____

   _____

   e. What did you learn about yourself in the process?

   _____

   _____

   f. What will you do differently in the future?

   _____

   _____

# 91

# Peer Coaching—From Problem to Opportunity

## Purpose

The purpose of the activity is to support students in empowering themselves to solve problems.

## Procedure

1. This activity may be used as particular problems arise or it may be done as a class activity. The sequence is similar to Activity 89, "Peer Coaching—Goals Update."

2. Distribute copies of the Peer Coaching—From Problem to Opportunity Worksheet.

3. Have each student find a partner and decide who will coach first.

4. Tell them to work on a problem that they are dealing with in their lives right now.

5. The coach asks the questions on the handout and records his or her partner's answers.

6. Allow 10–15 minutes, and then ask the students to switch roles and do the process again.

7. After another 10–15 minutes, call time. Have the students take a couple of minutes to share with their partners and express appreciation for the coaching.

8. Bring the students together into a full class circle and discuss the process, insights gained, questions still needing answers, problems solved, and students still needing support with their identified problems.

# PEER COACHING - FROM PROBLEM TO OPPORTUNITY WORKSHEET

1. What is the biggest *problem* you are dealing with right now?

_____

_____

2. What are the *specifics* of the situation?

_____

_____

3. What makes this a problem *for you?*

_____

_____

4. What *feelings* do you have in relation to this problem?

_____

_____

5. What aspects of the situation are within *your control* and which ones are not?

_____

_____

6. What is your *vision* of what you would like?

_____

_____

7. What is your *intention* in this area?

_____

_____

**8.** What specific *actions* will you take and when?

_____

_____

**9.** What *resources* or support do you need?

_____

_____

**10.** How *committed* are you to carrying out your plan and resolving this issue?

_____

_____

# 92

# *The Wisdom Within*

## *Purpose*

The purpose of this activity is to teach students how to work as a team to empower each other in solving their own problems. It reinforces the idea that often the solution to our problems can be found within ourselves.

The questions are based on a number of assumptions, many of which have been explored in other activities throughout the book. These principles include the following:

- Problems don't exist separately from someone's *experience* of the problem. Circumstances are the way they are. If I perceive them as a *problem,* that is a function of my interpretation.
- The notion of a *problem* almost always carries with it the belief that someone or something other than myself is the *cause* of the problem.
- The need to be right is to many people a stronger motivation than resolving the issue. (Almost all wars are demonstrations of this point.)
- The solution to just about any problem involves:

    —a willingness to take *responsibility* for solving it
    —a *vision* of what solutions are possible
    —a *commitment* to taking action.

## Procedure

1. Hand out copies of The Wisdom Within Worksheet and discuss the process with students before beginning.

2. Have the students form teams of six.

3. Have each team sit in a semicircle facing two empty chairs. One chair is for the student whose problem is to be solved. The other chair is for the "wise person within."

4. One student volunteers to be the first focus person. He or she sits in the first empty chair.

5. Other members of the team take turns asking the focus person the questions on The Wisdom Within Worksheet and listening as the focus person answers each question.

6. After the student has answered Question 10, he or she moves over to the other chair, which allows him or her to tap into his or her own inner wisdom. You might want to suggest that the student close his or her eyes for a moment, take a deep breath, and relax.

7. Once the focus student has taken a few seconds to access his or her inner wisdom state, then the group continues to ask the questions, numbered 11–20. Each question is asked by a different student in turn.

8. When the first student feels complete, a second student volunteers to be the next focus person. The process continues until everyone who wants to do it has had the opportunity.

9. We recommend that you move around from group to group to be available as a resource. Let the students know that if they get stuck and need help, you are available to assist. So as not to take the power away from them, avoid intervening in the process if the students are doing alright.

10. When everyone who wants to get support has finished, have the class reconvene in one large circle and discuss the process. Was it valuable? What did they learn from it?

## THE WISDOM WITHIN WORKSHEET

### Identifying the Problem

1. What is the problem or issue?

2. Specifically, what are facts of the situation?

3. What makes this a problem for you?

4. How are you interpreting the situation?

5. How are you feeling about this situation?

6. What are you saying is the cause of the problem?

7. What has prevented you from resolving this before now?

8. From your viewpoint, whose fault is it? Who is to blame? Who is wrong?

9. What are you being right about?

10. What is more important to you now—being right or resolving the issue?

### Empowering the Solution

11. Are you now willing to find a solution?

12. In what ways might you be contributing to the problem?

13. What could you do differently in the future?

14. What is your vision of how it will look, feel, or be?

15. How is this an opportunity for you to learn and grow?

16. How is it related to your purpose in life or in this area?

17. What do you not know about resolving this? If you did know, what would the solution be?

18. What specific actions will you take?

19. What resources or support might you need?

20. How committed are you to resolving this problem?

# 93

## Collaborative Problem Solving

> **D**on't find fault. Find a remedy.
>
> —Henry Ford

### Purpose

When conflicts arise between a couple of students, it is often best to let them work it out between themselves. This activity provides guidelines for arriving at win–win solutions through collaborative problem solving.

### Procedure

1. The concepts involved in this activity can be discussed with the class as a whole to set the stage for any particular problems that may arise.

2. Open the discussion in a manner similar to this: "What do all the following activities have in common?

   football games
   baseball games
   all professional sports

poker

Old Maid

all other card games (except solitaire)

most other game shows

grading systems in schools (sometimes)

court cases

political elections

war."

Let the students respond. If they get it, congratulate them. If not, say, "Each of these activities has winners and losers. The fact is, many activities in life are set up as win–lose situations. To be a winner, it seems, you have to defeat someone else. However, if you look at what makes a winning team, you notice that not only do they work together for a common goal, but they also care about each other. As each member grows in strength and ability, the entire team becomes more powerful. What this means is that there are no losers on a winning team. When problems arise, they are everybody's business. Solutions are found that allow each and every member to benefit." (Remember the lesson about the excess puzzle pieces? See Activity 87, "Every One Counts.") "You may be wondering if it is possible to have a game with no losers? Take a look and see."

3. Brainstorm typical problems that arise at school. For example,

- A guy is really attracted to a girl in his class but she seems to go out of her way to avoid him.
- Two girls practically grew up together but now they seem to be developing separate interests. One of them has taken to hanging around with a new group of friends. This group is involved in things the other girl does not respect, and she is feeling hurt and abandoned.
- A student has asked a classmate if he can copy her homework. She feels uncomfortable because she wants to help, but thinks it is unfair that she did all the work and he will get equal credit.

4. Select a couple of these problem areas to explore further.

5. Now brainstorm ways in which people on both sides of the issue would win; that is, get something they want.

6. Next distribute copies of the Collaborative Problem Solving Worksheet and have the students each fill one out based on the information generated from the problem situation that the class has been discussing.

7. Have students discuss the answers they wrote for each question and what value they got out of the exercise.

8. Indicate that this tool is available to them if problem situations arise in their own lives at school, at home, or at work.

## PROBLEM ANALYSIS—SELF

Identify a problem that involves someone else.

_____

_____

_____

Describe the situation in specific detail—separating *event* from *interpretation*.

What actually happened?                   What do you think it means?

_____        _____

_____        _____

_____        _____

What makes this a *problem* for you?

_____

_____

_____

How do you *feel* about it?

_____

_____

_____

What are you looking at as the *cause* of this problem? (Whose fault is it?)

_____

_____

189

# COLLABORATIVE PROBLEM SOLVING WORKSHEET (CONTINUED)

How would you like to see this *resolved?*

_____

_____

_____

_____

_____

_____

_____

_____

> *A* *problem well stated is half solved.*
>
> —John Dewey

# COLLABORATIVE PROBLEM SOLVING WORKSHEET (CONTINUED)

## PROBLEM ANALYSIS—OTHER

Is the other person *aware* there is a problem?

_____

_____

_____

What makes it a *problem* for him or her?

_____

_____

_____

How does he or she *feel* about it?

_____

_____

_____

What does he or she see as a *source* of the problem?

_____

_____

_____

How would he or she like to see it *resolved*?

_____

_____

_____

## PROBLEM RESOLUTION—JOINT

What is the larger *purpose* of this relationship or project?

_____

_____

_____

What areas of interest or concern do you have *in common*?

_____

_____

_____

How could you use this as an *opportunity* to further your purpose?

_____

_____

_____

How have you both *contributed* to the development of this problem?

_____

_____

_____

How could each of you *function differently* in the future to keep this problem from recurring?

_____

_____

_____

# COLLABORATIVE PROBLEM SOLVING WORKSHEET (CONTINUED)

What do you *want or need*, and how could the other person *support* you in getting it?

_____

_____

_____

What does the other person *want or need*, and how can you *support* him or her in getting it?

_____

_____

_____

Brainstorm possible *solutions* to the situation until you arrive at one in which both of you *win*.

_____

_____

_____

# 94

# Conflict Management

> **W**e have grasped the mystery of the atom, and rejected the Sermon on the Mount. . . . The world has achieved brilliance without conscience. Ours is a world of nuclear giants and ethical infants. We know more about war than we do about peace, more about killing than we know about living.
>
> —General Omar Bradley

## Purpose

In situations where the students who are involved in a conflict are unable to resolve it themselves, this activity will let them get assistance from peer conflict managers.

## Procedure

1. The steps in the conflict management process are outlined on the following pages. Review these with your students first.

2. Then set up a demonstration role-play involving two students in

conflict and four students serving as conflict managers. You may use the problem situations generated in the last activity, or decide on another.

3. Introduce the students to the process, step by step, allowing for any questions and observations as you go along.

4. Next, divide the class into groups of six and let them decide which two students will role-play the people who are in conflict and who will serve as conflict managers.

5. Select which conflict to use and have all groups working on the same one. Let them know that you are available as a resource if they need help.

6. When the groups are finished, bring them together for a class discussion. Find out how each group resolved the issue. Discuss the value of the process and how it can be used to resolve conflicts in the class, at school, at home, and in the community.

7. If there is enough interest and time, you may want to continue with these small group role-plays until everyone has had a turn and the skills of conflict management have been practiced until students have integrated them.

> *I want you to feel like loving your opponent, and the way to do it is to give them the same credit for honesty of purpose which you would claim for yourself.*
>
> —Mohandas Gandhi

# CONFLICT MANAGEMENT WORKSHEET

*Overview*

Step 1. Initiate the process (separate interviews).

Step 2. Define the problem (communication directed to conflict managers).

- Create environment.
- Gather information.
- Validate concerns and feelings.

Step 3. Expand awareness and understanding (direct communication between those with conflict).

- Listen to each other's experience.
- Restate to ensure mutual understanding.

Step 4. Resolve the conflict.

- Explore possible solutions.
- Select solution that is mutually agreeable.
- Confirm commitment to follow through.

Step 5. Complete the process.

- Hold a follow-up session.

*Detailed Process*

## STEP 1. INITIATE THE PROCESS:

- Meet separately with each party involved.
- Introduce yourself.
- Describe the process and your role as conflict manager.

    "The purpose of this process is to help you resolve the conflict. The way it works is, first you will tell me what happened from your point of view. While we are doing this, the other person involved in this conflict is describing his or her perception of what happened to another conflict manager.

    "Then we will bring you both together and let you tell each other your side of the story, including your feelings about what happened. Once you understand each other's points of view better, we will explore possible solutions on which both of you can agree.

    "My role is to facilitate communication and to help you two settle this issue."

- Explain the operating instructions:

    "For this process to work, you must agree to the following instructions:
    1. You are willing to use this process to resolve the conflict.
    2. You will use appropriate language (no cursing or swearing).
    3. You will behave appropriately (no threat of violence).
    4. Everything that is said is confidential.
    5. Conflict managers must report cases involving child abuse, pregnancy, and threats of serious violence.

- Get their agreement to cooperate

    "Do you agree to resolve the conflict by working with me through these five steps and to follow the operating instructions?"

## STEP 2. DEFINE THE PROBLEM:

- Review what you said to each of the parties separately, and confirm that each has agreed to resolve the conflict through this process.
- Explain that during this first part each person has a chance to talk about the situation without interruption, and he or she is to speak directly to you as the conflict manager.
- Determine who will speak first, and ask this person to explain what happened from his or her perspective.
- Use effective listening skills to help clarify everyone's understanding of this person's experience.
- Summarize what you've heard, and confirm for accuracy.
- Acknowledge and validate: "Thank you very much for describing your experience of this conflict. Given your perspective, I can appreciate how you feel."
- Repeat this part of the process with the other person involved in the dispute.
- Summarize both points of view, emphasizing similarities.

## STEP 3. EXPAND AWARENESS AND UNDERSTANDING:

- Determine who will speak first, and have this person communicate directly to the other person involved.
- Encourage this person to communicate responsibly, using "I" messages.
- Allow feelings and emotions to be expressed.
- To ensure understanding, have the other person restate what he or she heard.
- Summarize, validate, and acknowledge.

## STEP 4. RESOLVE THE CONFLICT:

- Ask each person how he or she would like to see the situation resolved.
- Explore possible solutions that would work for both of them.
- Decide on a solution that is:
  —specific
  —realistic
  —mutually satisfactory.
- Schedule a follow-up session to take place within a week.
- Have each person sign an agreement to implement the solution and to be at the follow-up session.
- Acknowledge their willingness to resolve this issue.

## STEP 5. COMPLETE THE PROCESS:

- Welcome everyone back.
- Review the purpose of this meeting and the issues involved in the conflict management process.
- Ask each person to share what has happened since the last session.
- Invite them to discuss what they learned through this process.
- If the issue has been resolved, acknowledge their success.
- If the issue remains unresolved, discover what didn't work and repeat steps in the conflict management process until a new commitment is made.

# CHAPTER EIGHT

# Community as Classroom

*L*et no one be discouraged by the belief there is nothing
one man or woman can do against the enormous array of
the world's ills—against misery and ignorance, injustice and
violence . . . few will have the greatness to bend history
itself, but each of us can work to change a small portion of
events, and in the total of all those acts will be written the
history of this generation. . . . It is from numberless, diverse
acts of courage and belief that human history is shaped.
Each time a person stands up for an ideal, or acts to
improve the lot of others, or strikes out against injustice, he
sends forth a tiny ripple of hope, and, crossing each other
from a million different centers of energy and daring, these
ripples build a current that can sweep down the mightiest
walls of oppression and resistance. . . .

Our future may be beyond our vision, but is not
completely beyond our control. It is the shaping impulse of
America that neither fate nor nature nor the irresistible tides
of history, but the work of our own hands, matched to
reason and principle, that will determine destiny.

—Robert F. Kennedy

# INTRODUCTION

*The most terrible poverty is loneliness and the feeling of being unwanted.*

—Mother Teresa

OPPORTUNITIES FOR LEARNING are not confined to classroom interactions. All of life has educational value. This chapter explores ways for students to take their new-found knowledge about responsibility into the world and to increase their wisdom as a result of their new experiences.

School, home, and the community at large are all presented as possible extensions of the classroom. The activities in this final chapter are meant to challenge tomorrow's leaders, to expand their sense of responsibility beyond the narrow limits of themselves and their group of friends to include the broader perspective of the rapidly changing, ever-shrinking global community.

## PEANUTS by Charles Schulz

Reprinted by permission of UFS, Inc.

## 95

# *Ideal School Vision*

## *Purpose*

This activity helps students expand their sense of responsibility beyond their classroom to the whole school.

## *Procedure*

1.  Begin this visualization using the standard set-up and relaxation process.

2.  Continue with the instructions provided here:

    • "Now that you are relaxed, continuing with your eyes closed, please imagine you possess a magic wand. And this magic wand gives you access to all the power and all the resources in the universe, so that you can create anything you want.

    • "If you could create your life exactly the way you wanted, how would it be?

    • "What would you be doing? How would you spend your time? What would your relationships with your friends and family be like?

    • "How would you feel about yourself? What would success look like for you? In what areas would you want to be successful?

    • "Moving beyond your personal situation, what would the world be like—if it were up to you? You have all the power and resources necessary to have the world be exactly as you want it, so how would you create it?" *(Give students a few minutes to silently consider this.)*

- "Now, in your ideal world, what would education or schooling be like? What purpose would it serve? What subjects would you study? Would there be schools, or in what other ways would learning take place? How would it feel to be involved in learning at your ideal school in your ideal world?" *(Pause.)*
- "How would education serve you and be related to your ideal life? What is your vision of your being successful at school?" *(Pause.)*
- "Is there anything else you notice about your ideal self, your ideal life, your ideal world and, in particular, your ideal school?" *(Pause.)*
- "Now begin to let go of anything that came up during this process, and—with your eyes still closed—begin to bring yourself back into the room."

3. Describe the room, making reference to how the room looks—details about the four walls, ceiling, floor, furniture, and so on, until you feel the students have returned to present time and are ready to open their eyes.

4. When the students have opened their eyes, give them a minute or so to stretch and then move into their support groups to share their experience.

5. Next, debrief this experience in a full circle by encouraging students to say what it was like for them. In particular, ask what their ideal school and vision of success in school looked like. On the chalkboard, list common elements in the students' visions.

6. Invite the students to identify a project they would like to take on that would be a positive contribution to their school, bringing it closer to their ideal vision. Develop an action plan for implementing this project successfully.

**LUANN** By Greg Evans

Reprinted with special permission of North America Syndicate, Inc.

# 96

# *Creative Decision Making*

## A Team Approach

## *Purpose*

A number of activities in this chapter involve brainstorming a list of possibilities and then deciding which ideas might be developed into action plans. The purpose of this activity is for students to learn a structure and skills for running meetings of this type effectively.

## *Procedure*

1. Tell the students that today they will be learning how to work together as a team to make effective decisions.

2. Hand out the Creative Decision Making Worksheet, and discuss the guidelines for running effective meetings.

3. Let the students know that they will have an opportunity to volunteer to serve as facilitators and recorders during the next series of activities.

4. Ask for a couple of students to volunteer now for the roles of facilitator and recorder in order for the class to practice running an effective meeting. You can do this with the full class or divide the students into three groups, each with their own facilitator and recorder.

5.  Hand out a copy of the Practice Agenda Worksheet and review the role of the facilitator and recorder in front of the group so that everyone understands what is to happen.

6.  Allow the students to run their meeting with as little direction from you as possible.

7.  At the end of the session, evaluate the process in the following way:

    • Ask the facilitator what he or she liked about the facilitation.
    • Ask the group what the facilitator did well.
    • Ask the recorder what he or she liked about recording.
    • Ask the group what the recorder did well.
    • Ask the group for other observations about what worked during the process.
    • Ask the group what didn't work and how it could be improved in future meetings.

## GUIDELINES FOR EFFECTIVE MEETINGS

- **Establish the Purpose of the Meeting.**
  Determine what the meeting is really designed to accomplish. In cases where a decision is to be made, be sure to reach a full understanding of the purpose the decision is meant to fulfill.
- **Set the Goal for the Meeting.**
  Be specific about the intended result, the desired outcome. At the end of the meeting, what tangible, concrete result will have been produced; for example, a list of options, an agreed-on decision, a plan of action?
- **Prepare an Agenda.**
  Consider *what* needs to happen in order to reach the desired outcome and *how* (through what process) this will be done. Think in terms of actions such as *present, brainstorm, select,* and *review.*
- **Determine Time Limits.**
  Estimate how long it will take to finish each item on the agenda.

## ROLE OF FACILITATOR

- Keeps the group focused on the process.
- Encourages participation from everyone.
- Listens, accepts, and validates everything that is said without judgment.
- Makes suggestions about the process.
- Makes sure the recorder can keep up.
- Asks someone to keep track of the time.
- Does not contribute his or her own ideas about the topic.

## ROLE OF RECORDER

- Writes what is being said on newsprint or butcher paper so that everyone can read it.
- Uses key words and phrases from group members.
- Invites the group to let him or her know if something is recorded inaccurately.
- Does not contribute his or her own ideas regarding the topic.

## ROLE OF GROUP MEMBER

- Contributes ideas.
- Supports the process.
- Listens to and respects others' ideas.
- Honors time limits.

## OPERATING INSTRUCTIONS FOR BRAINSTORMING

- All ideas are accepted and appreciated. (There are no right or wrong, better or worse contributions.)
- Be creative.
- Build on other people's ideas.
- Defer evaluation or judgment until later.
- More is better. (Come up with as many ideas as you can.)

## SELECTION PROCESS

- After brainstorming, check for understanding of ideas.
- Eliminate duplications.
- Everyone votes for their top three choices. (The choices can be weighted as follows— first choices get three points, second place two points, and third preference gets one point. The item with the greatest number of points is considered the best choice.)

## SUCCESS CRITERIA

- In cases where the voting does not indicate an obvious choice or in really important situations, establish by what criteria a successful solution will be measured.
- List and agree on the criteria that will meet the group's needs, given the purpose of the decision.
- Evaluate possible choices against these criteria.

## Topic: Classroom Recognition Program

### Purpose

The purpose of this meeting is to enhance how we all feel about participating in this class.

### Goal

Decide on a plan and a procedure for recognizing students who make a positive contribution during this next week.

### Agenda

- Review and agree on purpose, goal, agenda, and operating instructions. 5 min.
- Brainstorm ideas for class recognition program. 5 min.
- Review and refine list, rank order, and select. 5 min.
- Develop action plan (what, how, who, when). 5 min.

# 97

# School Operating Instructions

## *Purpose*

This activity can help students deepen their understanding of responsibility by giving them an opportunity to teach these principles to other students, to develop their leadership skills, and to promote greater responsibility throughout the school.

## *Procedure*

1. Discuss with your students the idea of working with other classes in the school to develop a set of operating instructions. Have interested students volunteer to participate.

2. Review the guidelines for facilitators and recorders with the students who are to be involved, and have them design a lesson on responsibility based on their experience in this class.

3. Arrange for students to present their lessons to other classes for the purpose of having these other students agree on a set of operating instructions for themselves.

4. Explore with other staff and school administrators the value of schoolwide operating instructions. If enough interest exists, discuss a process for developing such instructions.

One possible approach is to have a student representative from each class bring class operating instructions to a "constitutional convention." As a collective body, they can then develop a list for the school, which could include instructions for the playground, cafeteria, and so on.

Note that in contrast to school rules, which tend to be stated in negative terms, operating instructions describe what to do to make it work. It is the difference between "No weapons are allowed on campus or you will be expelled" and "Respect everyone's right to learn in a safe school environment."

# 98

# Schoolwide Acknowledgment Program

## Purpose

The purpose of this activity is to create a more positive environment at the school by recognizing students who make a difference.

## Procedure

1. Discuss with your students their experience of the acknowledgment activities done in this class, and explore the value of a schoolwide recognition program.

2. Using the model for creative decision making practiced in the previous activity, brainstorm possible ideas for acknowledgment activities that could work for the entire school. Some suggestions are included here.*

3. Have them select the ideas that seem most feasible and develop a plan for making them happen.

---

*The authors wish to thank the California Association of Student Councils and their member schools for providing these suggested activities.

Contributed by
McAuliffe Middle School
Riverside, CA

## STAFF APPRECIATION WEEK

The leadership class uses the week before winter vacation to show the staff how much they are appreciated.

The faculty lounge is decorated for the season. A wooden chimney or fireplace was placed in the lounge and a stocking was labeled for each member of the staff. (Stockings were hung from the chimney with care.)

Each day, the stockings were filled with different little gifts for the staff members. If an object was too big to fit into the stocking, a note was placed in the stocking telling the staff that the surprise was in the mail box.

The week culminated with a faculty-staff breakfast in the school's multipurpose room. In addition to the school's faculty and staff, personnel from the district office, past officers, and PTA officers were also invited.

The leadership class decorated the room, purchased the food and the utensils, organized the seating arrangements, and handled all the introductions. As a special treat, the high school show choir provided the entertainment.

Parents volunteered their time to help cook the breakfast, and we were able to use the school's cafeteria.

This is a great way to show the staff how much they are appreciated, and it's a wonderful way to end what is usually a very hectic week for all.

Contributed by
Don Robinson
Potter Jr. High School
Fallbrook, CA

## STAFF APPRECIATION AND STUDENT–FACULTY RELATIONSHIPS

Every year, members of our school's leadership class and selected staff members participate in a "Secret Pals" gift exchange the two weeks prior to winter vacation. The program is strictly voluntary and has proven to be extremely successful in helping to develop student–faculty relations.

Members of the leadership class develop a questionnaire, as do members of the faculty, that asks pertinent questions about the particular interests of each group. A random drawing takes place in the leadership class, and each student selects a questionnaire that has been filled out by a staff member. The staff member then receives the questionnaire written by the same student that chose his or her questionnaire.

**212**

All questionnaires are anonymous so that neither party knows the identity of the other. The class advisor assigns a number to each pair of Secret Pals, and this number is used in all correspondence. Students bring in messages and small gifts on a daily basis to a designated location, usually a box located in the advisor's office or classroom. The advisor acts as a "go-between," taking gifts to the staff members and relaying their gifts to the students.

Care is taken to keep both sides from learning the identity of their Secret Pals. Staff members are asked to type or print all correspondence and should keep all gifts out of sight, away from the eyes of inquisitive students.

At the end of the two-week period, a special get-together is arranged. Refreshments are served by members of the leadership class, and each person in attendance gets to find out the identity of his or her Secret Pal.

Students and faculty find this experience very rewarding. Most participants sign up year after year. It is a nice way to get ready for the holidays.

## Secret Pal Questionnaire (staff)

1. Are you male or female?
2. What do you do in your spare time?
3. What is your favorite sweet?
4. What kind of music do you enjoy? What is your favorite group?
5. What is the craziest thing you have done on a date?
6. What was the dumbest thing you did in school?
7. If you could travel anywhere in the world, where would it be and why?
8. If you won the grand prize in the lottery, what is the first thing you would buy?
9. If you could change anything about your life, what would it be?
10. Where were you born, and what is your earliest memory?
11. What's your idea of a great weekend?
12. If UPS delivered a surprise package to you, what would you like to have in it?
13. What's the first thing you notice about a person?
14. Who was your "hero" when you were young?
15. What was your most embarrassing moment?
16. What are your impressions of today's students in this school? (Tell the truth!)

---

Contributed by
Analy High School
Sebastapol, CA

# SECRET PAL PROGRAM

The Secret Pal program started at Analy High School several years ago. This program pairs teachers and staff members with unknown Secret Pal students. Throughout the year gifts, notes and cards are exchanged. At the end of the year we hold a barbecue in one of the local parks. School Board members cook the meal and the rest is potluck. At this barbecue, Secret Pals are revealed to the staff members and gifts are exchanged.

The program has been very positive and was a winner of the Association of School Administrators Award for a positive school program to improve the school climate.

The organization is as follows: A student signs up to be a Secret Pal and is paired with a staff member. Both the teacher and the Secret Pal fill out forms listing their likes and desires, favorite gifts, candy, and so forth. It asks about their hobbies on both forms also, so that both faculty member and student have a list about their Secret Pal. Secret Pals are not known to the staff members and are only revealed at the end of the year.

This has been a very positive program to promote positive relationships between the students and the faculty, and has helped to develop a warmer relationship between teachers, staff, and students at our high school.

### Secret Pal Survey

Please answer all the questions and return it as soon as possible.

When is your birthday?
What are your favorite hobbies and interests?
What are some of your main personal interests?
What is your favorite food or candy?
Are there any special activities you enjoy doing alone?
Are there any special activities you enjoy doing in groups?
Are you allergic to anything? If so, what?
What brightens your day?
What is your favorite color?
What kind of music do you like? What artist(s)?
What is your favorite holiday?
What is your favorite movie?
Who is your favorite author?

---

Contributed by
Cindy Mazanet, Director of Student Activities
Helen Estock School
Tustin, CA

## COFFEE CART

Once a month, selected members of the student council and the principal take around a small decorated cart and serve coffee, tea, and muffins to the teachers and all the staff.

The cart is usually decorated to denote the holiday of that particular month: green and white shamrocks for St. Patrick's Day, red hearts for Valentine's Day, and so on. Teachers and all the staff look forward to the coffee cart!

_____

Contributed by
David Herber, Roberta Heter, Activity Directors
Lompoc High School
Lompoc, CA

## STUDENT SPOTLIGHT

This is the second year now that our student council has had a Student Spotlight. The Student Spotlight committee chooses one student a month. They take a picture and have an 8 × 10 black-and-white glossy made. They interview the student and do a write-up, which is posted with the photograph on a specially marked area of a bulletin board in the cafeteria.

The idea stemmed from wanting to make the student body more aware of some of the things kids on our campus are involved in. The committee tries to select students who may not be well known or always in the "news," but who are active in some area of campus life. The write-up also may include information about off-campus areas of interest.

Included in our "spotlights" have been a first-year majorette, a soccer player, an honor band member who is also a varsity athlete, and an athlete who is involved in drama.

The choice is up to the committee, but they seek recommendations from students, counselors, teachers, and so on.

_____

Contributed by
Thomas Jefferson Jr. High
305 Griffiths
Wasco, CA

## COUGAR OF THE MONTH PROGRAM

At Thomas Jefferson School, we have a Cougar of the Week program to honor students with outstanding citizenship qualities. They are honored in the local paper, and so on. From the Cougars of the Week, we choose a Cougar of the Month for each grade level. These students' pictures are placed in the office display case. We contract with our local photography studio to make us an 8 × 10 black-and-white photo of each student. Students keep their pictures once the next month's students are chosen. From the Cougars of the Month, we chose three Cougars of the Semester—one per grade level. These students have color pictures taken by the studio (8 × 10), displayed in a separate area. This makes a very unique and memorable experience for these students as well as the community.

Contributed by
Barbara Marinos, Activities Director
Somerset Junior High
Modesto, CA

## NO STRANGERS AT SOMERSET

At Somerset Junior High we try very hard to make new students feel welcome. After a new student enrolls, chooses subjects and is tested, he or she is dismissed for the day. He or she returns the following morning and is given a schedule and a student "buddy" who takes the new student on a campus tour, explains schedules, lockers, nutrition break, school rules, and so on. Following the tour, the student is brought into the leadership class and introduced to the officers and class. The new student's schedule is read, and any student in any of his or her classes raises his or her hand and introduces him- or herself. The student in the leadership class then becomes a "buddy" for that class or lunch. He or she then takes over the new student in that class, introduces him or her to the teacher and class and adds some background information. The new student is given a "Welcome to School" pencil, a Tiger pencil, and a free gift certificate to the Tiger Trader, our student store. One of our goals in leadership is to make the new student feel the Tiger Spirit and become a friend.

Contributed by
Martin Luther King Middle School
Seaside, CA

## STUDENT RECOGNITION

### Procedures for Selecting Student of the Month

Each month a department will highlight its students. Please follow the procedures outlined below.

1. Choose one student from each of the classes you teach in the department of the month.
2. Fill out the attached form and return to the principal.
3. Students will be photographed. Photos will be given to the teacher. An area in the classroom should be designated for display of students' pictures.
4. Certificates will be issued to the teacher. Please make an introduction in each class as you present certificates.
5. A letter will go home from the administration.

6. A bumper sticker that reads, "My Child Was Student of the Month at King Middle" will be sent home.
7. At the end of the month, send photos to the office for a display in the office.
8. The department highlight order is listed here:

| Month | Department | Date Selection Form to the Principal |
| --- | --- | --- |
| February | Art | January 28 |
| March | Business | February 23 |
| April | Foreign Language | March 25 |
| May | Home Economics | April 24 |

## Student of the Month Selection Form

MONTH _____

DEPARTMENT _____

TEACHER _____

Please complete this form by selecting students on the following criteria:

- CLASS BEHAVIOR—attitude, courtesy, and respect
- RESPONSIBILITY—citizenship, initiative, and responsibility for self
- SERVICE—to the class and/or school
- SELF-ESTEEM—displays self-confidence, feels self-worth
- ACHIEVEMENT—achievement according to ability or shows improvement

| Students | Grade | Period |
| --- | --- | --- |
| _____ | _____ | _____ |
| _____ | _____ | _____ |
| _____ | _____ | _____ |
| _____ | _____ | _____ |
| _____ | _____ | _____ |

Return this form to the principal by your department's due date.

Contributed by
Bob Russel, Activities Director
Pacific Grove High School
Pacific Grove, CA

## ACADEMIC TRIVIA WEEK

For one week each teacher is given an amount of "Breaker Bucks" money that the activity director produces, with the faces of faculty and staff on it. The duplicating machine and colored paper can do wonders!

Each teacher is told to give the "Breaker Bucks" for outstanding academic achievement or for some special academic trivia contests within the classroom.

During the week at lunchtime we hold schoolwide trivia contests where students can earn more "Breaker Bucks." On Monday we have world history trivia for the 9th grade; Tuesday, English literature trivia and a special math puzzle contest; on Wednesday we hold a U.S. history trivia contest for juniors, and on Thursday an economics–government contest for seniors.

By this time there are thousands of dollars floating around campus (beware the student who attempts to counterfeit!), yet you will not find one bill on the ground, for on Friday we have our academic trivia auction, where students can bid their money for prizes. Some students will pool their money and others will not. The auction will need people to take and count the cash and give away the prizes. I've found the food prizes were more desired than such things as sweatshirts and T-shirts. Six-packs of Coke, McDonald's coupons, and quarts of malted milk balls were really big items, either free or at minimum expense.

Teachers said that the students really worked to gain the bucks, and it was a very highly motivational program. We do this in April, the normally slower part of the year just before prom preparations.

One warning . . . after the last gift is auctioned there will be bucks still floating around . . . we had thousands thrown into the air, en masse, after the end of the auction . . . it made it very festive!

218

# 99

# *Parents as Partners*

## Responsibility Begins at Home

*If* there is righteousness in the heart, there will be beauty in the character.

If there be beauty in the character, there will be harmony in the home.

If there is harmony in the home, there will be order in the nation.

When there is order in the nation, there will be peace in the world.

—Chinese proverb

## *Purpose*

This activity elicits support at home for activities promoting student responsibility.

## Procedure

1.  Discuss with your students which activities done as part of this class might have application for them at home. One school where we worked, for example, had a sheet that was sent home to parents that included:

    - the school's purpose
    - the school's operating instructions
    - the particular student's goals
    - a place for the parents to identify their goals in support of their child's success
    - a place for the parents to write a statement of commitment to support their child's success at school.

2.  Decide whether it will be a class project where all students will do the same activity or whether each student is welcome to pick the ones they want.

3.  Identify ways in which the students can support each other with their family projects.

# 100

# Community-Based Projects

> **W**e are not going to be able to operate our
> Spaceship Earth successfully for much longer
> unless we see it as a whole spaceship and our fate
> as common. It has to be everybody or nobody.
>
> —Buckminster Fuller

## Purpose

This activity helps students to become actively involved in contributing to their community.

## Procedure

1.  Using the creative decision making process, brainstorm possible community-based projects that your class or school might implement. (Some suggestions are provided).*

---

*Thanks again to the California Association of Student Councils for these ideas.

2. Select one that the group could realistically accomplish.

3. As a way of structuring the process, you may want to use the Project Management Worksheet, which adapts some of the guidelines presented in Chapter Six.

4. Consider whether academic credit for student involvement seems appropriate. If so, you might discuss with them what projects might provide the greatest opportunity to learn academic skills such as math (a fundraising event), English (a letter-writing campaign), history (a multicultural experience), physical sciences (an environmentally related project), social sciences (working with senior citizens, the underprivileged), and so on.

Establish a way of documenting the learning—perhaps an independent study contract—in order to award credit for work done on the project.

Contributed by
Ed Railsback, Director of Activities
Paso Robles High School
Paso Robles, CA

# ASSOCIATED STUDENT BODY COMMUNITY PROJECT

## Leadership Class Community Project

This year, as part of their class requirements in leadership, each student must plan, coordinate and complete a community project. The project must benefit the community at large or any specific segment of the community. The project can be in the form of a fundraiser, a service, or a support for some other philanthropic community group.

The major criteria for each project are as follows:

- Each project has a specific purpose.
- Each participant must be committed to seeing the project through completely.
- Each project must involve as many others as possible.
- Each project must be evaluated and a written report submitted on its completion.

This year's projects vary both in scope and in length. They include:

- a schoolwide canned food drive
- restoration of picnic tables and children's cubbyholes and the planting of flowers at the Children's Center on Oak Park
- an Adopt-a-Grandparent program at a local convalescent home
- specific presentations and cookie making for the Paso Robles Co-op Preschool
- a schoolwide drive to collect toys for the local needy families in conjunction with other city groups
- a planned participation in the March of Dimes Mothers' Walk in March or April
- a carwash to raise funds for the local homeless shelter
- a luncheon for people at the Paso Robles Convalescent Home.

Each project will use the various organizational and leadership skills taught in the leadership class curriculum and experienced through the responsibilities assumed when executing student activities.

I want to make sure that each of you understands what is expected from you concerning your community projects. I hope that the following list will help. *But remember—this list may or may not be everything that is needed. It is only some suggestions. You will need to use your judgment.*

1. Have a specific purpose for what you are doing. Write it out and try to achieve that purpose during the project.

2. Talk to other individuals or groups to better understand how you can achieve your purpose. Don't assume that you have the only way to do it.

3. Coordinate your project with the proper community group if that is appropriate. Try not to duplicate efforts, but do try to coordinate.

4. Each individual in a group must have submitted a form explaining the project. Each should be equal partners in the effort.

5. A detailed evaluation and report on your project will be *due on* _____ or no later than *one week* after completion of the project. This is a must *from each member* of the project committee. (Report forms will be available at a later date.)

6. Once you commit to a project, you must see it through. Failure to do so will make you and the leadership class look very poor. It will also result in a dramatic lowering of your grade.

7. Get others involved—do not rely only on yourselves. You are the leaders—the catalysts, if you will. You must organize and coordinate the project to involve others. *Spread the good feeling that you'll get from this project to others.*

8. Search deep inside yourself and ask if you are doing your very best to make this project work. What's your answer? If it is *yes!* then you will find a lot of goodwill and personal satisfaction from your efforts!

GOOD LUCK!

Contributed by
Linden High School
Linden, CA

# ORGANIZING A HIGH SCHOOL BLOOD DRIVE
# FEEL GOOD ABOUT YOURSELF—GIVE BLOOD

Blood cannot be manufactured. Only people can give this precious gift of life. Patients who need blood to enhance the quality of their lives depend on volunteer blood donors like yourselves. Within our five-county community, we serve patients in 19 hospitals who use 3,000 units of blood each month.

Annually, we must recruit more than 34,000 donors. We rely on our high school blood program for many of these new faces. Once donors are recruited, we must collect, test, store, and deliver their blood to 19 hospitals daily.

High school students play a vital role in assuring that patients who need blood actually get it. Every student 17 years and older may donate at the blood drive. Until you are 17, working at the blood drive provides various opportunities to get involved. You will find that serving as donors, recruiters, and volunteers offers a unique way to touch other people's lives.

## When Do We Start? Suggested Time Table

As chair and co-chair, you will need to coordinate blood drive plans with your volunteers, the Delta Blood Bank consultant and school faculty. Be aware of all aspects of the drive and see that assigned jobs are carried out.

*4 weeks prior:*

1. Hold initial planning meeting.
2. Select committee chairperson.
3. Start publicity campaign.
4. Make sure site is confirmed for blood drive.

*3 weeks prior:*

1. Start recruitment campaign.
2. Put out articles in school newspaper.

*2 weeks prior:*

1. Start visiting individual classes.
2. Put sign-up tables in cafeteria, at games or school functions.

*1 week prior:*

1. Begin daily PA announcements.
2. Return sign-up sheets to recruitment.
3. Start scheduling appointments.

*2 days prior:*

1. Call Delta Blood Bank to report total number of sign-ups and confirm unloading help.
2. Send out pre-screening slips with appointment times.

*Day of drive:*

1. Have room unlocked and cleared prior to Delta Blood Bank's arrival.
2. Meet head nurse and give him or her the appointment schedule.

*After drive:*

1. Return site to normal condition.
2. Thank everyone who participated.
3. Deliver follow-up article to school newspaper.
4. Follow through with recognition activities.

## Committee Structure

Be ready to organize the Bloodmobile Committee five weeks before the drive date. Committee structure is the essential element in a successful campaign—appoint key people as chairs. Each committee may have the following (if your group is small, two positions may be held by the same person):

**Chair and Co-chair:** Select a senior and junior for these positions to assure continuity and leadership for future drives. Must have responsible, committed students. These people will call and chair committee meetings.

**Recruitment Chair:** Will be responsible for scheduling donors at regular, specified intervals and preparing a final master schedule.

**Publicity Chair:** Lots of energy, time and creativity are needed to carry out this job. The chair is responsible for publicizing the blood drive to students, parents, staff, and faculty and developing recognition events so donors and volunteers feel appreciated.

**Volunteer and Operations Chair:** These students are responsible for reserving and setting up the site for the blood drive. This committee will help unload and reload the Delta Blood Bank truck. They will recruit students to be trained to work during the blood drive.

**The Bloodmobile Committee's** first meeting should be held about 4 weeks prior to the blood drive. Since this is a planning meeting, use the following checklist.

_____ Your Delta Blood Bank Consultant, faculty advisor, and all committee members should be invited to this meeting.

_____ Be sure mobile site is reserved for day and hours needed.

_____ Chair and co-chair explain duties of each committee.

_____ Individual chairs gather names for their committee.

_____ Make assignments now for individual recruiters who will be going from class to class speaking and recruiting. Set deadlines for:
- distributing sign-up sheets
- returning sign-up sheets
- mailing out reminder cards
- putting up posters
- getting out publicity
- completing the appointment schedule.

_____ Review recruitment procedures with Delta Blood Bank consultant.

_____ Distribute donor sign-up sheets, posters, all materials.

PROJECT MANAGEMENT WORKSHEET

## DESCRIPTION OF PROJECT

_____

_____

_____

## PURPOSE OF PROJECT

_____

_____

_____

## GOALS OF PROJECT (BE SMART)

_____

_____

_____

## ACTION STEPS

| *What* | *Who* | *By When* |
|---|---|---|
| | | |
| | | |
| | | |
| | | |
| | | |

# PROJECT EVALUATION WORKSHEET

NAME OF PROJECT/EVENT _____

EVALUATOR _____ DATE OF PROJECT/EVENT _____

EVALUATOR WORKED IN THE FOLLOWING CAPACITY ON THIS PROJECT ____

_____

Keep in mind that a person trying to organize this project will be reading this next year. The more information that you can give to this person, the more smoothly this project should run. If you need more paper, attach a sheet.

1. Make a list (in detail) of the things you had to do prior to this event to make this project go. Include approximate times with reference to the date of the event (*example:* one week before the event, you need to order flowers). Be specific. Who did you have to talk to? What kind of arrangement did you make for a room? (and so on).

2. What needs to be done during the event?

3. What materials were needed for this project? Include how to pick them up, where to get them, and how to order these items.

| *Materials* | *Quantities* | *Costs* | *Suppliers' Names and Telephone Numbers* |
|---|---|---|---|
| | | | |

_____

4. How many people were on your committee?
   Do you suggest more or fewer people for the next time this project is run? Why?
   What were the various duties of the people on your committee?
   Did your committee function smoothly? Why or why not?

5. Are there any suggestions that you could give for next year's group?

6. What did *you* learn from being involved in this project or event?

## 101

# We Are the World

> **R**emember that you are all people and that all people are you.
>
> —Joy Harjo

## Purpose

This activity is meant to expand students' global awareness.

## Procedure

A number of different activities can be used to achieve this purpose:

### 1. Exploring Your Cultural Heritage

Have students research their ancestry and prepare a report on their cultural heritage including country origins, food, music, art, and customs. This could be expanded into a multi-cultural fare with a pot luck of ethnic foods, singing songs in different languages, and so on.

## 2. Pen Pals

Students can identify parts of the world about which they would like to learn more and write to pen pals in those countries. A letter to the editor of the local newspaper is a good way to make contact. Writing to people serving in the military in that area is another option.

## 3. World Travelers

- Students are invited to prepare an itinerary for a world tour. They can get maps and select which cities and countries they will visit. They can go to a travel agent and collect posters and brochures of their various destinations. They can study languages, cultures, customs, and money systems. They can interview people who have been there to get ideas for places to go and things to do.
- Students then prepare a report on their planned trips. They can work in groups if they want to travel together.
- This could be used as an entire unit, with academic credit given for different aspects of the project.

## 4. World Leaders

You can ask the students to imagine that they have an opportunity to meet with all the world's leaders. Have the students prepare a presentation that they would give to those leaders about what kind of world they envision and any suggestions that they have for realizing their vision.


After either of the preceding activities, read the following quotation from Norman Cousins and ask the students to identify all the things that people from all over the world have in common.

*T*his is the confession of a half-educated man. My education prepared me superbly for a bird's-eye view of the world; it taught me how to recognize easily and instantly the things that differentiate one place or one people from another. But my education failed to teach me that the principal significance of such differences is that they are largely without significance. My education failed to grasp the fact that beyond the differences are realities scarcely comprehended because of their shattering simplicity. And the simplest reality of all is that the human community is one—greater than any of its parts, greater than the separateness imposed by actions, greater than the divergent faiths and allegiances or the depth and color of varying cultures.

—Norman Cousins

Permission courtesy of Penguin USA.

# THE FAR SIDE

By GARY LARSON

"Mr. Osborne, may I be excused? My brain is full."

# RESOURCES

What follows is a listing of the books, tapes, and organizations we have found helpful in our journey to greater responsibility both in our own lives and in our classrooms. You are encouraged to immerse yourself in the context of responsibility through books, tapes, and seminars, so that you may become a more powerful and effective educator.

## 1. Books for Educators and General Interest

BEDLEY, GENE. *The Big R: Responsibility*. Irvine, Calif.: People-Wise Publishers, 1985.

BYHAM, WILLIAM. *Zapp! The Lightning of Empowerment*. New York: Harmony Books, 1988.

COVEY, STEPHEN. *The Seven Habits of Highly Effective People*. New York: Simon & Schuster, 1989.

CURWIN, RICHARD L., AND ALLEN N. MENDLER. *Discipline with Dignity*. Alexandria, Va.: Association for Supervision and Curriculum Development, 1988.

EMERY, STEWART. *The Owner's Manual for Your Life*. Garden City, New York: Doubleday, 1982.

ENRIGHT, JOHN. *Enlightening Gestalt*. Mill Valley, Calif.: Protelos, 1980.

FRITZ, ROBERT. *The Path of Least Resistance: Learning to Become the Creative Force in Your Own Life*. New York: Fawcett Columbine, 1989.

GIBB, JACK. *Trust: A New View of Personal and Organizational Development*. Los Angeles: The Guild of Tutors Press, 1978.

GLASSER, WILLIAM. *Control Theory in the Classroom*. New York: Harper & Row, 1986.

GLENN, H. STEPHEN, AND JANE NELSEN. *Raising Self-Reliant Children in a Self-Indulgent World: Seven Building Blocks for Developing Capable Young People*. Roblin, Calif.: Prima Publishing, 1988.

LABORDE, GENIE Z. *Influencing with Integrity*. Palo Alto, Calif.: Syntony Publishing, 1987.

NEWMAN, JAMES W. *Release Your Brakes!* New York: Warner, 1977.

PURKEY, WILLIAM WATSON, AND JOHN NOVAK. *Inviting School Success*. Belmont, Calif.: Wadsworth, 1984.

235

ROBBINS, ANTHONY. *Unlimited Power: The New Science of Personal Achievement.* New York: Simon & Schuster, 1986.

STEVENS, JOHN O. *Awareness: Exploring, Experimenting, Experiencing.* New York: Bantam, 1973.


## 2. Books We Recommend for Parents

CLEMES, HARRIS, AND REYNOLD BEAN. *How to Discipline Children Without Feeling Guilty.* Los Angeles: Price Stern Sloan, 1978 and 1990.

CLEMES, HARRIS, AND REYNOLD BEAN. *How to Teach Children Responsibility.* Los Angeles: Price Stern Sloan, 1978 and 1990.

DINKMEYER, DON, AND GARY D. MCKAY. *Raising a Responsible Child.* New York: Simon & Schuster, 1973.

GORDON, THOMAS. *Teaching Children Self-Discipline . . . at Home and at School: New Ways for Parents and Teachers to Build Self-Control, Self-Esteem, and Self-Reliance.* New York: Times Books, 1989.

MARSTON, STEPHANIE. *The Magic of Encouragement: Nurturing Your Child's Self-Esteem.* New York: William Morrow, 1990.

NELSEN, JANE. *Positive Discipline.* Fair Oaks, Calif.: Sunrise Press, 1981.


## 3. Books and Curricula for Additional Classroom Activities

BORBA, MICHELE. *Esteem Builders: A K-8 Self-Esteem Curriculum for Improving Student Achievement, Behavior and School Climate.* Rolling Hills Estates, Calif.: Jalmar Press, 1989.

CANFIELD, JACK, AND HAROLD WELLS. *100 Ways to Enhance Self-Concept in the Classroom.* Englewood Cliffs, N.J.: Prentice-Hall, 1976.

CANFIELD, JACK, et al. *Self-Esteem in the Classroom: A Curriculum Guide.* Self-Esteem Seminars, 6035 Bristol Parkway, Culver City, CA, 90230: Self-Esteem Seminars, 1986 and 1990.

DEMBROWSKY, CONNIE. *Affective Skill Development for Adolescents.* Available from Connie Dembrowsky, P.O. Box 67001, Lincoln, NE 68506.

DURFEE, CLIFF. *More Teachable Moments.* San Diego, CA: Live, Love, Laugh, 1983. This is a wonderful curriculum on communication skills.

MOORMAN, CHICK, AND DEE DISHON. *Our Classroom: We Can Learn Together.* Englewood Cliffs, N.J.: Prentice-Hall, 1983.

PALOMARES, UVALDO, and others. *The Human Development Program.* Spring Valley, Calif.; Magic Circle Publishing, 1970. This is the famous "magic circle program," which is a great curriculum for teaching communication skills and emotional maturity.

REASONER, ROBERT. *Building Self-Esteem.* Palo Alto, Calif.: Consulting Psychologists Press, 1982.

SICCONE, FRANK. *Responsibility: The Most Basic 'R.'* San Francisco: Siccone Institute, 1987.

SICCONE, FRANK. *Teacher as Coach.* San Francisco: Siccone Institute, 1988.

SICCONE, FRANK, ed., *The Best of Self-Esteem.* San Francisco: Siccone Institute, 1990.

## 4. Guided Imagery and Relaxation

DAVIS, MARTHA, ELIZABETH ROBBINS ESHELMAN, and MATTHEW MCKAY. *The Relaxation and Stress Reduction Workbook.* Richmond, Calif.: New Harbinger, 1980.

DEMILLE, RICHARD. *Put Your Mother on the Ceiling: Children's Imagination Games.* New York: Viking Compass, 1973.

HENDRICKS, GAY, AND RUSSELL WILLS. *The Centering Book.* Englewood Cliffs, N.J.: Prentice-Hall, 1975.

HENDRICKS, GAY, AND THOMAS B. ROBERTS. *The Second Centering Book.* Englewood Cliffs, N.J.: Prentice-Hall 1977.

NICHOLS, EUGENE. *Picture Yourself a Winner.* Lakemont, Ga: CSA Press, 1978.

SHERMAN, HAROLD. *How to Picture What You Want.* New York: Fawcett/Goldmedal, 1978.

## 5. Organizations That Can Help You

ALLIANCE FOR INVITATIONAL EDUCATION, c/o Mary Snyder, Room 216, Curry Building, University of North Carolina, Greensboro, NC 27412. Write for membership information.

CALIFORNIA ASSOCIATION OF STUDENT COUNCILS, 1212 Preservation Park Way, Oakland, CA 94612.

CENTER FOR SELF-ESTEEM, P.O. Box 1532, Santa Cruz, CA 95060. Sponsors the Annual California Self-Esteem Conference.

FOUNDATION FOR SELF-ESTEEM, 6035 Bristol Parkway, Culver City, CA 90230 (Jack Canfield, president). Sponsors an annual Southern California Self-Esteem Conference.

NATIONAL COUNCIL FOR SELF-ESTEEM, P.O. Box 277877, Sacramento, CA 95827. *This is a national membership organization dedicated to promoting the development of self-esteem and personal responsibility in schools. Write for a free newsletter and application form. We are both on the board of trustees of this organization and highly recommend membership. NCSE sponsors numerous national and regional conferences.*

SELF-ESTEEM SEMINARS, 6035 Bristol Parkway, Culver City, CA 90230.

*(Jack Canfield, president) Conducts workshops and in-service trainings in the areas of self-esteem, peak performance, and responsibility training. Write for a copy of their free newsletter and educational materials brochure. They also distribute the STAR (Success Through Action and Responsibility) program for school administrative staff.*

SICCONE INSTITUTE, 2151 Union Street, San Francisco, CA 94123.

*Offers training and consulting services in the areas of education, business and personal development. In-service workshops are available for administrators, teachers, students, and parents in areas including educational leadership, self-esteem and responsibility, communication and teamwork, and teacher as coach. Write for information.*